# THE
# WEALTH
# WITHIN

## SYMBOLISM OF THE THORN
## AND ROYAL CROWNS

THE THORN CROWN symbolizes the false identity the world (Satan) imposed on Jesus. It was a symbol of mockery and a means of causing pain. When the Roman soldiers called Jesus "the king of the Jews," they were diminishing His worth, though He is the King of Kings—the eternal King. This thorn crown represents our old, sinful nature that was crucified with Jesus. It signifies the carnal mindset that must be renewed with Gospel truth.

In contrast, the royal crown symbolizes the new creation—our new nature recreated in Christ after the image and likeness of God. It signifies our true identity in Him—an identity Jesus ascribed to us when we became one with Him on the cross, taking on His nature as ours. This new identity encompasses sonship, royalty, righteousness, redemption, and more. This royal crown represents the mind that is continuously being renewed, the mind that mirrors the mind of Christ—the wealth mindset.

Jesus bore our sin so we can become righteous!

He took on our fallen (false) identity so we can embrace our true identity in Him!

He assumed our dishonor so we can have His worth!

**He wore the thorn crown so we can wear the royal crown!**

# THE WEALTH WITHIN

## RENEWING YOUR MIND TO LIVE FROM THE ABUNDANCE OF GOD'S KINGDOM

### Lewam Hailu

Cover Design: Jonathan Lewis and Mekdim Desta
Interior Design: Jonathan Lewis
Editing: Katherine Talpos and Abbey McLaughlin

ISBN: 979-8-9911336-0-9 (Paperback)
ISBN: 979-8-9911336-1-6 (Hardcover)
ISBN: 979-8-9911336-2-3 (eBook)

# Dedication

I dedicate this book to those who pursue excellence of mind and believe in endless possibilities. To those who dare to dream with God and carry God-given visions, this is especially for you!

# Acknowledgments

I would like to extend my deepest gratitude to my wonderful husband, Henok Tesfaye. Your unwavering support and willingness to be my sounding board have been invaluable. Thank you for believing in me and my vision.

To Schlyce Jimenez, your guidance launched me into my God-given purpose and set me on the path to write this book. Your initiation was a pivotal moment in this journey.

To Susan King, your prayers and encouragement have been refreshing. Thank you for seeing my potential and my unique expression of Christ. The laughter and humor we shared along the way taught me the value of light-heartedness in life.

To Ken Powell, your readiness to help and elevate my book has been exemplary. Your insights and feedback have been significant. Thank you for honoring my work.

To Mekdim Desta, your creativity and generosity have been a blessing.

# Contents

# Preface

I HAVE LONG been passionate about the issue of poverty and the disparity in living standards. While some relish a life of luxury, enjoying the finer things of life, others struggle to provide the basics for their families. Still, others find themselves in the middle—having enough but not sufficient for significant strides in life. I often pondered how people end up where they are—whether it is a result of their choices (self-imposed), influenced by others (other-imposed), externally driven by forces beyond their control, or divinely orchestrated. Such questions stirred my thoughts often.

Little did I know that my curiosity was a God-given desire on the issue, guiding me to discover my calling and pursue my divine purpose. These inclinations served as indicators, pointing me toward the problems I was meant to solve for others. My own struggles along the way became a bridge connecting me to the hearts of those facing similar challenges and who would benefit from my acquired knowledge and wisdom. I have been on a continuous journey of learning and growth in this area because, as the saying goes, you cannot teach others what you do not know yourself. By aligning my gifts and passions of faith, entrepreneurship, social impact, and poverty alleviation, I endeavored to create Kingdom solutions. I had no idea how they would all beautifully come together.

The journey of writing this book began in June 2017 with a significant dream. *Yes, you heard me right!* Dreams are one of the primary ways God communicates with me, but this one was unique! In the dream, I found myself in a classroom with a few other students discussing the topic of poverty with Jesus, who was the teacher. In response to a question Jesus asked, "What is poverty?" two peers gave their answers, and just as it was my turn, I woke up. Despite finding it strange, I was certain God was prompting me toward a meaningful task, though the specifics were not clear. To my surprise, the very next day, I had a similar dream; this time, Jesus instructed us to write a paper on poverty with a clear deadline of one week.

These vivid dreams are etched in my memory, serving as a clear confirmation and the initial clue that my long-standing passion for poverty solutions might be more than just an interest; it was a God-given focus leading me to a meaningful purpose. Perhaps God's hand had been guiding me all along.

> Poverty is a complex interplay of hope, belief, and the absence of a dream or vision—essentially, a mindset.

Following the instruction, I immersed myself in researching poverty, delving into Scripture, and seeking understanding and wisdom in God's presence. The topic, while fascinating to me, presented its own set of challenges. The sheer vastness and complexity left me grappling with where to begin.

Through this wrestling process, a profound realization dawned on me. Poverty, at its core, is not *merely* a financial problem. It is a complex interplay of hope, belief, and the absence of a dream or vision—essentially, a mindset. *Poverty,*

*I concluded, is a mindset!* While many external factors are at play outside of our control, our internal makeup (the invisible and intangible force behind the scenes) emerges as the determining factor. Poverty is a mindset that manifests in many ways, with finances just one of them. It became evident that one could be financially affluent yet impoverished mentally in reality.

Even when faced with external factors like negative microeconomic conditions, natural disasters, injustice, poor governance, lack of education, and financial illiteracy—many of which are beyond one's control—I discovered an abundance of evidence and countless stories of people who overcame similar circumstances. It became evident that one's mindset was still the game-changer—how people perceived themselves, their situations, their ability to overcome challenges, and their optimistic hope for the future. Regardless of the external factors causing poverty in the physical realm, a person's mindset and belief system play a pivotal role in determining whether they remained in a state of lack. God unmistakably guided me through this process, and I sensed I was uncovering something significant.

> **Regardless of the external factors causing poverty in the physical realm, a person's mindset and belief system play a pivotal role in determining whether they remained in a state of lack.**

Recognizing this, I focused my paper (the one assigned from the dream) on addressing the root cause—*a poverty mindset*—understanding that tackling the source prevents the outcome. God was unmistakably guiding my steps through this process, and I sensed I was uncovering something significant.

Soon after, another revelation hit me. If a negative and limiting belief system constituting a poverty mindset causes people to remain in lack, a positive and healthy mindset—*a wealth mindset*—stands as the antithesis and solution to releasing people from the problem.

What intrigued me even more was the realization that mindsets, be it poverty or wealth, are pervasive across both believers and unbelievers alike. Some non-believers possess a wealth mindset, albeit limited, without knowing Christ. Conversely, many Christians, despite their knowledge of Christ—the ultimate Source—find themselves entrenched in a poverty mindset. That was a sobering realization! This insight struck me profoundly, fueling my determination to confront the issue within the Christian community.

Armed with this fresh wisdom and insight, I pressed on with my paper. The outcome? A robust twenty-page document that not only met the deadline (yes, I met it!) but also later became the foundational blueprint for the book you are about to read. Beyond the satisfaction of completing the paper, I was astonished by the depth of understanding I gained about the subject.

With the completion of the project, I found myself asking, "What is next, God? What do I do with this paper?" Expecting a clear instruction, I was met with surprising silence. A puzzling situation, leaving me wondering about the significance beyond a mere paper. In the absence of further divine instruction, I discerned it was time to set it aside.

Now that my eyes were opened and my spirit awakened to the truths of poverty and wealth mindsets, God continued to teach me more. In the subsequent years, He unfolded profound revelations and deep understanding, eventually shaping the wisdom within the pages of this book.

Without much warning, God dropped a bombshell a few years later: I was meant to write a book. Immediately, I knew the theme it was to be! After all, He had prepared me in advance, leading me to compose the blueprint. The call was clear—it was time to revisit the paper, unravel its layers, and transform it into a book. Confirmation came through other people, further solidifying the path ahead.

With a clear plan in sight, it was time to partner with the Holy Spirit to breathe life into the blueprint. I co-authored this book with Him, translating the lessons He imparted to me into teachings for others. Though the task seemed daunting, and I initially felt unqualified, excitement eventually overcame hesitation. I knew I was equipped and ready to start the project.

Despite feeling overwhelmed, I began the preparation process in obedience. God paved the way, providing the means and connections necessary for this assignment. Like many believers entrusted with divine assignments, I encountered opposition from all sides—health challenges, mental and emotional attacks, hindrances, and even persecution from those around me.

The opposition was intense, but I pressed on. God's presence and grace accompanied me, keeping my joy and peace intact. The enemy trembled at the thought of this book's release, fearing that his lies would be exposed. Readers were going to be freed from a poverty mindset, no longer limited by their wrong beliefs and negative thought patterns. Instead, a journey of experiencing heaven's abundance and its unlimited possibilities awaited them. The outcome? A transformation into Kingdom-minded individuals—a major threat to the enemy.

Within these pages, you will discover the wisdom I have acquired on my journey with God—through the highs and lows and in the mountaintops and valleys. I share revelations and insights born in the quiet and intimate times in His presence. I reveal the mind renewals and transformations I have experienced as I spent time in His word, learning and contemplating His ways and thoughts. Brace yourself for the mind-blowing goodness of the gospel that possesses the power to renew your mind and transform your life as it did mine. It holds the ability to uproot any scarcity mentality and shift your perspective, leading you to live confidently in the provision and abundance of God. Remember, poverty in all its forms is a curse, and the cross has already dealt with it!

> "Christ redeemed us from the curse of the law by becoming a curse for us—for it is written, 'Cursed is everyone who is hanged on a tree.'" (Galatians 3:13, ESV)

> "For you know the grace of our Lord Jesus Christ, that though He was rich, yet for your sakes He became poor, that you through His poverty might become rich." (2 Corinthians 8:9 NKJV)

In my own journey, I have witnessed the profound impact of the gospel—transforming me spiritually, mentally, emotionally, and even financially. It serves as a constant reminder that God is always engaged in the business of redeeming and restoring lives. What never ceases to amaze me is that, whether in the "promised land" of success and blessings or navigating the challenging "wilderness" of difficulty and unfruitfulness, God consistently provides.

**Poverty in all its forms is a curse, and the cross has already dealt with it.**

Think of the wilderness as a transitional space, a necessary passage on our way to the promised land. By design, it is a temporary place of preparation and refinement as we cooperate with God through the process. Remember, it is not intended to be our permanent abode; resist the temptation to settle in the wilderness, circling the same mountain as the Israelites!

In the wilderness, our identities are refined and developed, preparing us to carry our purpose into completion and steward the abundance in the promised land. It is a place for intimate encounter with God and His ways, guarding our affection and devotion to Him from the allures of the blessings ahead. More importantly, it is a place of taking off the "old" and putting on the "new"—shedding old thinking patterns and beliefs and embracing gospel truth.

Today, make the decision to renew your mind and adopt a Kingdom mindset of abundance, propelling you toward your destiny and a purpose-filled life. Personally, I have committed to continually renewing my mind and excelling in a wealth mindset. *How about you?* Will you commit to confronting any ingrained limiting beliefs and disrupting poor thinking patterns? This is a movement of radical believers who, by faith, opt for a life of excellence and abundance in the Kingdom and actively influence the world around them!

Will you join me in this movement?

# Sleepwalking Through Life

YOU WERE NOT meant to live this way. A wealth mindset is your inheritance!

We are all familiar with the concept of the "American Dream." It is not simply a notion we have heard and aspired to at some point; we have all found ourselves entangled in its web. When coined in 1931, the original vision created dreams of equality, justice, and democracy for everyone in the nation. Initially, it aimed to provide a life of equal opportunities based on abilities or achievements, envisioning a life of betterment, prosperity, and fulfillment for all.

However, over the decades and across generations, the term "American Dream" has undergone a noticeable evolution. In recent times, the term has been repurposed, and its focus has shifted toward the pursuit and accumulation of individual wealth—emphasizing the prospect of attaining success (particularly in financial terms). While there is nothing inherently wrong with aspiring to and

> You were not meant to live this way. A wealth mindset is your inheritance!

attaining financial success and independence (actually, it is golden), this pursuit has unintentionally ensnared many of us in the form of invisible (yet very real) bondage.

In this endless and futile pursuit, we find ourselves entangled in a lifestyle marked by fiercely competitive routines, all driven by the desire to get ahead financially. While the primary intent is to provide for ourselves and our families, we unknowingly give into an insatiable human appetite for more. Not only does this lifestyle prove to be unpleasant, unfulfilling, monotonous, and draining, but it also leaves little room or time for genuine enjoyment of life—both in the company of loved ones and in savoring the fruits of our hard work. We lose the opportunity for much-needed rest and overall well-being.

As we fall into this trap, we find ourselves ensnared in the relentless cycle of a hamster wheel—constantly busy, yet never accomplishing anything truly important or meaningful. In this pursuit, we unknowingly cheat ourselves out of a fulfilling, abundant, and meaningful life: *a life of true significance*. We forfeit our God-given purpose in life and exchange our visions and dreams for money and material possessions. We slave away, toil, and trade our blood, sweat, and tears to gain or stay in financial security. We live in constant stress of financial concerns, fear of instability, and perpetual worry about inadequacy or an uncertain future. We unintentionally become slaves of the prevailing economic system or, should I say, conforming to the world standard. We become prisoners of the dollar bill. And sadly, many within the body of Christ still find themselves entrenched in this modern rat race.

However, for the believer, there exists a superior way—the Kingdom's way! The Kingdom of God is not meant to be a distant, future, elusive, ever-seeking, or unattainable realm. It transcends being a mere theological concept; rather, it is a profoundly real, tangible, and vibrant reality. Despite its invisible nature, it is a present reality—not confined to a future occurrence. As a born-again believer, you are already living in the Kingdom. It is already within you, an intrinsic part of your current existence.

God longs for you to understand, be conscious of, and fully engage with the Kingdom—embracing its ideals, culture, rights, and privileges. He longs for you to be fully alive within the Kingdom, calling you to personally encounter its abundance and release its transformative presence and influence into the world around you.

Many of us find ourselves stuck in the one-dimensional, visible world where rationality, logic, and intellect rule our lives. We lack awareness of the higher and greater spirit realm that we already carry within us, a realm "superimposed" on and coexists with this physical world. So many of us struggle to comprehend how to actively engage and activate this spiritual dimension in our lives, and I was no exception. Over time, I not only discovered how to engage with the Kingdom but also learned to live in alignment with its realities, which often stand in contrast to the world's standards. The journey begins with a shift in mindset and an awakening to its profound realities.

> **The Kingdom of God is not meant to be a distant, future, elusive, ever-seeking, or unattainable realm.**

In the pages of this book, I aim to impart the revelation knowledge and wisdom I have gained about renewing the mind with the gospel truth so that you are equipped to begin living from the abundance of God's Kingdom. Together, we will explore the concept of a wealth mindset through the lens of the Kingdom and uncover practical ways to cultivate and nurture it in your life.

I intend to reintroduce you to the nature of God and redirect your focus to your true identity in Christ. With this renewed understanding, you will be better positioned to avoid the shackles of the world's system and escape the relentless rat race. Rather than slaving away, toiling, and grinding, you will find the opportunity to engage in work that is productive, meaningful, and fulfilling (with eternal significance)! You can live a purpose-filled life where dreaming and pursuing your God-given vision are not only encouraged but celebrated.

I aim to help you rethink and redefine your perception of and relationship with money, urging you to adopt a Kingdom mindset. In doing so, you will find freedom from being bound, bullied, and controlled by the power of money. When you align your mindset (beliefs and thought patterns) with Kingdom values, money becomes an inevitable *by-product* of knowing and walking in your identity in Christ (Matthew 6:33), marked by the pursuit and fulfillment of your visions and dreams. It becomes a tool meant to serve you rather than an idol to be served. This shift in perspective redirects your focus away from money itself and toward the endless possibilities in the Kingdom and the pursuit of your life's purpose.

> **When you align your mindset with Kingdom values, money becomes an inevitable *by-product* of knowing and walking in your identity in Christ, marked by the pursuit and fulfillment of your visions and dreams.**

I intend to show you that you no longer have to navigate life out of fear and worry regarding finances, even amid life's storms and economic challenges. Instead, you can start to experience God's perfect peace, joy, and rest by gaining revelation knowledge of His abundant provision, regardless of your external circumstances.

The emphasis of this book is not on achieving financial prosperity or accumulating wealth; rather, it is on seeking and advancing God's Kingdom first and foremost through the renewal of our minds. True biblical prosperity is a function of seeking God, aligning ourselves with Kingdom perspectives, and fulfilling our unique purpose. Rather than a narrow concentration on a wealth mindset solely in financial terms, we will broaden our scope to encompass all facets of life. The wisdom imparted can be applied universally, spanning in areas like relationships, parenting, work, and business.

This book does not endorse "get rich quick" schemes or a "prosperity gospel" that promise effortless benefits with minimal effort, time, and risk. Similar to any biblical principle, cultivating a wealth mindset requires discipline in renewing our minds with the truth of the gospel, actively engaging our faith that manifests in actions, and maintaining patient endurance, especially when immediate results are not evident.

> True biblical prosperity is a function of seeking God, aligning ourselves with Kingdom perspectives, and fulfilling our unique purpose.

Although important, this book does not deal with acquiring skills like financial management. Without a renewed mind, skills such as saving, budgeting, and investing alone fall short of creating a lasting impact. True transformation, as emphasized in this book, stems from shifting our perspectives and beliefs with Kingdom truth through the power of the Holy Spirit. Our inward reality shapes our outward experience.

Besides, the mere acquisition of financial information and skill sets devoid of faith is incomplete and ungodly. I am referring to faith in God—our Source of provision—and not faith in our money management skills, which is misplaced faith. Faith is the currency of the Kingdom! For the believer, faith is how we engage with the spiritual realm and access every promise and blessing from God. Without faith, it is impossible to please God (Hebrews 11:6). Faith is a function of a renewed mind, a result of a transformed belief system originating from revelation of truth.

**Our inward reality shapes our outward experience.**

## THIS BOOK IS FOR YOU IF YOU DESIRE TO

1. Grow in intimacy with God, discover your identity in Christ, and adopt a Kingdom mindset.
2. Realize your dreams and visions, embrace endless possibilities, and become a solution in the world while building a legacy that brings the essence of God's Kingdom on earth.
3. Position yourself to receive God's abundance, financial or otherwise, recognizing that this abundance is intended for a purpose greater than yourself. It is designed for advancing His Kingdom and spreading the gospel.
4. Lead a life free from financial fear, stress, and worry, regardless of your external circumstances, and aspire to live a life of child-like trust in God marked by peace, joy, and rest.

## HOW THIS BOOK IS ORGANIZED

This book is divided into three parts: Mindsets, Renewal, and Experience.

In *Mindsets*, I lay out the compelling argument for the profound impact of our thoughts on our life's trajectory, drawing insights from biblical wisdom. We discuss how our dominantly formed thought patterns and belief systems constitute either poverty or wealth mindsets. Our journey continues by discussing a poverty mindset, dissecting its many components, revealing its nature, and detailing its symptoms. Subsequently, we explore the concept of a wealth mindset, unraveling its essence and tracing its origins while also shedding light on its manifold manifestations.

Moving on to *Renewal*, we embark on the actual process of renewing our minds with truth, propelling us toward cultivating a wealth mindset. We will first explore the gospel and its foundational role in nurturing this mindset. We then study the significance of knowing God and His character, emphasizing its part in embracing a mindset of wealth. Furthermore, we look at the profound impact of knowing and living in our authentic identity in Christ, which is a crucial element in fully operating with this mindset. Lastly, we uncover the liberating truths surrounding giving and money, allowing us to view them through a different lens that reframes our perception and frees us to embody a wealth mindset fully. Throughout this part, you will encounter truths and revelations that will wash away any remnants of poverty thinking, launching you into a successful journey of mind renewal.

> **Faith is the currency of the Kingdom . . . It is a function of a renewed mind, a result of a transformed belief system originating from revelation of truth.**

Finally, in *Experience*, we bring our journey full circle by concluding with an overarching truth that encapsulates the essence of a wealth mindset. We part ways by outlining practical ways to apply this mindset across all facets of life, ushering you to experience its many rewards.

## MY DESIRE FOR THIS BOOK

I earnestly hope and pray that with every page you turn in this book, you will gain the wisdom, clarity, and confidence you need to identify and confront any poverty mindset and old thinking patterns that hold you down and tie you to a worldly system.

Simultaneously, I trust that you will find the courage and inspiration to adopt a wealth mindset that embodies and exudes the principles and realities of the Kingdom. While mind renewal is a life-long process, the earlier you embark on this path, the sooner you will reap its benefits and enjoy a life of abundance.

Let's get started!

PART 1

# MINDSETS

———

## CHAPTER 1

# The Power of Thoughts

"Watch your thoughts, they become your words; watch your
words, they become your actions; watch your actions, they
become your habits; watch your habits, they become your
character; watch your character, it becomes your destiny."

LAO TZU[1]

AS I REFLECT on the profound wisdom in this quote, a vivid
memory arises from several years ago when I initially realized
the influence my thoughts held in shaping both my present
reality and the trajectory of my destiny. At first, I struggled
to believe this idea; I even dismissed it entirely. I thought,
"Surely, God is in control of my life. My thoughts and words
cannot possibly have that much power over my life to dictate
its course." It took a great deal of time for me to fully embrace
this truth and, over the years, I have resolved to learn and
better understand it.

I even examined all areas of my life to see what was thriving and what needed improvement. Upon closer inspection, I

was pleased with the realization that my thoughts and words were contributing positively to the successful areas. Yet, it was sobering to acknowledge my responsibility for the areas that were facing challenges.

I prayerfully processed this truth with God and asked Him to reveal the specific thought patterns and mindsets contributing to the negative experiences in my life. In His gentle and kind way, He brought them to the surface and, as I reflected, I could not deny their truth. I realized I had unknowingly held these negative thought patterns, shaping my life in an unintended manner. Quickly, I repented, changing my mind about those negative beliefs, and sought God's truth to replace them. And so, my journey with thoughts began!

> Our mindsets—the firm, deeply-seated, and strongly formed thoughts and belief patterns—run our lives behind the scenes.

Our thoughts—the ones that are persistent and linger, and *not* the random and fleeting ones that pass through our minds and disappear—form patterns that eventually become a mindset. Put simply, a mindset is a collection of beliefs, perceptions, and perspectives about ourselves, others, God, and life in general. It is the lens through which we view the world. It plays a significant role in influencing our attitudes, decisions, and behaviors. In essence, it dictates the way we think, feel, and behave, with our feelings and behaviors often traceable back to our thoughts. Our mindsets—the firm, deeply-seated, and strongly formed thoughts and belief patterns—run our lives behind the scenes. They are what psychologists commonly refer to as the subconscious mind.

Whether we realize it or not, our mindsets play a defining role in shaping our life experiences and are often the architects of our present circumstances. The positive ones breathe life into our journey, fostering success, flourishing relationships, and a positive self-image. Conversely, the negative ones hold a destructive influence, steering us toward failure, strained relationships, and diminished self-esteem. Even our perceptions of God significantly impact our relationship with Him—shaping how we interact with Him, the depth of our love and trust for Him, and our ability to receive from Him. Our mindsets are so powerful that they intricately mold the course of our lives, for the better or worse.

> **Our mindsets are so powerful that they intricately mold the course of our lives, for the better or worse.**

This goes beyond mere science or psychology; it is certainly not some version of positive thinking or a new-age concept. It is very much in alignment with the timeless wisdom of God's word. Scripture consistently emphasizes the significance of our thoughts and words in shaping who we are and our life experiences, whether we will live the abundant life that Jesus intended for us. The abundant life is, first and foremost, an inner reality.

## A BIBLICAL PERSPECTIVE ON MINDSETS

While the Bible does not explicitly use the term "mindset," it provides several teachings and principles that offer insight into the importance of our thinking and perceptions. Consider this psalmist's prayer: "May these words of my mouth and **this meditation of my heart** be pleasing in your sight, LORD, my Rock and my Redeemer" (Psalm 19:14, NIV, emphasis added). Here, the psalmist actively monitors and assesses the thoughts occupying his mind, ensuring their acceptability in the sight of God.

In his profound wisdom, King Solomon teaches us, "As a man thinketh, so is he" (Proverbs 23:7 KJV). In simple terms, this implies that our thoughts shape who we are. It suggests that our innermost thoughts and beliefs mold our true character and intentions. Building on this wisdom, Proverbs 4:23 (NIV) further advises, "Above all else, guard your heart, for everything you do flows from it." This emphasizes the importance of protecting our hearts—our inner world of thoughts and emotions—as they influence our actions.

The Bible also characterizes these wrong or negative thought patterns as lies of the enemy, which we unknowingly accept and believe as truth. Sometimes, they are referred to as strongholds, which are strongly held destructive beliefs. When Jesus called the devil the "father of lies," He emphasized that lies and deception are the devil's native language (John 8:44). These lies can pertain to God, ourselves, our life circumstances, and others.

These lies manifest under the disguise of consistent fears and worries about issues in our lives. They also take the form of deceptive stories and narratives conceived in our minds, often suggested by the enemy. Sometimes, they are reflected as interpretations we invent to make sense of events and circumstances in our lives without seeking God's perspective, thereby allowing the enemy to inject his negative ideas and interpretations. They also manifest as unfounded negative assumptions about others, lacking true discernment and detrimentally impacting relationships. In essence, any thoughts, ideas, and imaginations contrary to God's truth are lies from the devil. This is precisely why Scripture guides us to actively dismantle them.

"The weapons we fight with are not the weapons of the world. On the contrary, they have divine power to demolish strongholds. **We demolish arguments and every pretension that sets itself up against the knowledge of God, and we take captive every thought** to make it obedient to Christ." (2 Corinthians 10:4-5, NIV, emphasis added)

In the realm of spiritual warfare, where believers are urged to put on their armor and stand firm against the devil's schemes (Ephesians 6:11-12), the mind becomes the greatest battlefield. It is where the enemy strives to establish a foothold, a space in our heads that influences our mindsets and belief systems in opposition to God's truth. Whoever controls the mind (a highly strategic position) essentially holds control over one's life...until exposed and brought into the light.

> **Whoever controls the mind (a highly strategic position) essentially holds control over one's life.**

In this battlefield of the mind is also where our fight lies: either preoccupying it with God's truth or reclaiming territory that was under the enemy's control.

## THE CHURCH AND MINDSETS

Historically, the church has predominantly concentrated on addressing external behaviors, actions, and outward sins—all visible aspects of a person's life. Unfortunately, this approach has often resulted in mere behavior modification without real transformation within, and such modifications are inherently unsustainable. External manifestations are not the root causes or issues. They only represent symptoms of what lies within our thought patterns and beliefs—namely, our mindset. Without resolving the underlying problem, symptoms are prone to resurface frequently in different forms. As Jesus teaches,

"'What comes out of a person is what defiles them. **For it is from within, out of a person's heart, that evil thoughts come**—sexual immorality, theft, murder, adultery, greed, malice, deceit, lewdness, envy, slander, arrogance and folly. All these evils come from inside and defile a person.'" (Mark 7:20-23, NIV, emphasis added)

Consider this scenario: a believer relying on their efforts to cleanse themselves from sin (an external behavior) has not been established in the truth that Jesus has become their righteousness (an inner belief). As a result, they still identify themselves as an ongoing sinner (not past), thereby placing dependence on their self-righteousness. This person will most likely continue to struggle with different expressions of sin. In contrast, a believer who understands and embraces Christ's righteousness as their own, firmly rooted in their identity as the righteousness of God in Christ and as a saint, will exemplify a life of obedience reflected in righteous thinking and living (2 Corinthians 5:21).

Therefore, the prevailing focus within the church on external behaviors and visible sins, leading to surface-level changes rather than real transformation, needs to shift to one that celebrates authentic and holistic transformation that begins within and shapes our mindset, ultimately influencing our outward conduct.

## RENEWING THE MIND

Indeed, true transformation comes from the inside out. Spiritual maturity takes place when we consciously shift our old thought patterns and dispel erroneous beliefs through the power of the Holy Spirit. This process is described by the Apostle Paul in Scripture as the "renewing of the mind":

"Do not conform to the pattern of this world, but **be transformed by the renewing of your mind.** Then you will be able to test and approve what God's will is—his good, pleasing and perfect will." (Romans 12:2, NIV, emphasis added)

Fascinatingly, this concept is subtly woven throughout Scripture, emerging unexpectedly in teachings about repentance. The Greek term for repentance, *metanoia* (μετάνοια), literally translates to changing one's mind or perspective. Dr. Francois Du Toit, author of *The Mirror* Study Bible Translation, describes this phrase as a combination of two words: *meta*, meaning "together with," and *noieō*, meaning "to perceive with the mind." Du Toit further describes it as "the awakening of the mind to what is true; a realignment of one's reasoning, a gathering of one's thoughts, and a co-knowing."[2] This unveils the profound nature of repentance, emphasizing a transformative shift in perception and a harmonizing of thoughts—a co-mingling of our thoughts with God's thoughts.

The term "repentance" is predominantly used in the New Testament, particularly in the messages of Jesus and John the Baptist, to point the Jews to the introduction of God's Kingdom, signifying the fulfillment of the old covenant. They preached, "'Repent, for the kingdom of heaven has come near'" (Matthew 4:17, NIV). In this context, they urged Jews to shift their minds from the old order of things and adopt the new order of the gospel (see Matthew 3:2 and Mark 1:15).

This understanding of repentance significantly differs from the historical teachings of the church and the views of many religious leaders. Repentance was viewed as an endless activity of apologizing and seeking forgiveness, showing feelings of guilt and shame as an explanation for bad behavior, and pleading with God to turn away from a life of sin. According to *The Mirror* Bible, the Greek term *metanoia* has no connection with the Latin term *paenitentia*, from which penance originates, which means self-inflicted payback and punishment. True repentance involves a transformative shift in our minds through the revelation of truth.

As we wholeheartedly embrace genuine repentance and renew our minds, we actively substitute our thoughts with God's thoughts and align our ways with His. In the words of the Lord,

> "For my thoughts are not your thoughts, neither are your ways my ways, saith the LORD. For as the heavens are higher than the earth, so are my ways higher than your ways, and my thoughts than your thoughts." (Isaiah 55:8-9, NIV)

Let us intentionally cultivate a mindset that mirrors His, recognizing the vast difference between His ways and thoughts and ours.

Renewing the mind involves adopting a mind that is governed by the Spirit, which yields life and peace, while intentionally rejecting the carnal mind that is governed by the flesh, which leads to "death" (Romans 8:6). A Spirit-controlled mind directs its focus toward "whatever is noble, whatever is right, whatever is pure, whatever is lovely, [and] whatever is admirable" (Philippians 4:8, NIV, emphasis added). It is a recognition that we already possess the Spirit of self-control and a sound mind, empowering us to cultivate such thoughts (2 Timothy 1:7).

Mind renewal is not a mental exercise; it differs from mere introspection or self-reflection, which are self-led endeavors. This transformative process occurs in collaboration with the Holy Spirit, who intimately understands the deep-seated issues and thought patterns within our hearts. It surpasses Bible memorization and empty declarations that are devoid of revelation and faith. Instead, it entails the Holy Spirit revealing God's truth and His nature, which serve as the mirror that reflects and informs our true identity. Mind renewal is an ongoing, life-long process that demands intentional and consistent efforts grounded in reliance on God, leading to breakthroughs in every facet of life.

> **The quality of our internal thought life intricately shapes the quality of our eternal life. An excellent mind produces an excellent life!**

Therefore, as mature sons of God who are led by the Spirit, let us make every effort to advance and excel in the practice of renewing our minds. May we cultivate thoughts, attitudes, and beliefs of excellence. The quality of our internal thought life intricately shapes the quality of our eternal life. An excellent mind produces an excellent life!

## GOD'S SOVEREIGNTY AND OUR THOUGHTS

If you are anything like me at the beginning of this journey, you may still grapple with the idea of our thoughts and belief systems shaping our lives, especially when we believe in God. *Is God not in control?* Surely, Scripture teaches that God is sovereign over all things. You might wonder if that is a contradiction. The answer is no! I firmly believe God is *not* in control of everything—especially not our thoughts, decisions, and actions. We have control over our thoughts and actions. We have a role to play through our agreements (our yeses and amens) and deciding whether to align ourselves with His thoughts and ways. We are active participants along with God in this journey called life and His divine plan.

While God may not control every detail, He is undoubtedly in charge and absolutely sovereign. He has the final say! In His sovereignty, He intervenes and steps into our human conditions and weaknesses, orchestrating them for our good and His glory (Romans 8:28). Every circumstance becomes a tool in His hands to fulfill His plans and purposes. He makes His grace—His supernatural enabling—available to us so we are *not* left to navigate on our own without any help.

**We are active participants along with God in this journey called life and His divine plan.**

John Crowder captures this essence of God's sovereignty:

"If your idea of sovereignty involves God single-handedly causing everything, then you have collapsed God into creation—a reprehensible monism that posits all human evils and atrocities as actions and therefore attributes of the divine nature. That said, He does sustain all things and leaves nothing to mere chance (or ultimately up to you). Evil does not have its own autonomy...In Jesus Christ, we see that God is not the bringer of evil, but the redeemer from evil. He allows our liberty, foreseeing our error, with the rescue, redemption and restoration of humanity summed up in Christ from before our very creation."[3]

However, God's sovereignty does not exempt us from personal responsibility. Our free will remains intact, giving us the choice to follow Christ, partner with Him, and agree with His perspectives. It is crucial to also acknowledge the presence of an adversary, the devil, seeking to steal, kill, and destroy—determined to influence our thoughts, distort our beliefs, and rob us of our faith. This is why we are encouraged in 1 Peter 5:8 (ESV) to "**Be sober-minded; be watchful.** Your adversary the devil prowls around like a roaring lion, seeking someone to devour" (emphasis added). Let us, therefore, exercise our free will, making choices that bring glory to God.

In *Mere Christianity*, C. S. Lewis masterfully delves into the concept of free will and its role in the existence of evil in light of God's sovereignty:

"God created things which had free will. That means creatures which can go wrong or right. Some people think they can imagine a creature which was free but had no possibility of going wrong, but I can't. If a thing is free to be good, it's also free to be bad. And free will is what has made evil possible. Why, then, did God give them free will? Because free will, though it makes evil possible, is also the only thing that makes possible any love or goodness or joy worth having. A world of automata—of creatures that worked like machines—would hardly be worth creating. The happiness which God designs for His higher creatures is the happiness of being freely, voluntarily united to Him and to each other in an ecstasy of love and delight compared with which the most rapturous love between a man and a woman on this earth is mere milk and water. And for that they've got to be free. Of course, God knew what would happen if they used their freedom the wrong way: apparently, He thought it worth the risk."[4]

> Every circumstance becomes a tool in His hands to fulfill His plans and purposes.

## PARTNERING WITH GOD

As in every aspect of our Christian walk, the process of renewing the mind operates as a partnership between us and the Holy Spirit. This means we should not attempt to *independently* address our thought life in an effort to alter our negative life circumstances. Understanding that our mindset plays a role in the negative outcomes of our lives is not intended to instill fear or anxiety, causing us to strive and work hard on our own to achieve desired results. Simultaneously, we are not *passive* bystanders waiting for God to miraculously change all our circumstances (at least as mature believers).

> Abiding in God's presence through prayer allows His thoughts to envelop our minds and souls. His presence has the power to wash over any distortion in our thinking.

While there are usually no instant fixes to life's myriad problems and challenges, sometimes we can bring about rapid shifts in our beliefs and mindsets and usher in breakthroughs without needless delays. Striking a healthy and appropriate balance is key. So, what does this partnership between us and the Holy Spirit entail?

In our active engagement in the renewal of our minds and the transformation of our lives, the most important aspect is to trust and find rest in the assurance that we have a Good Shepherd overseeing our lives. We are not alone. Abiding in God's presence through prayer allows His thoughts to envelop our minds and souls. His presence has the power to wash over any distortion in our thinking. An integral part of this transformative journey involves actively engaging the Holy Spirit to illuminate His light in our specific circumstances, seeking His insight and perspective. This requires staying connected to

His voice, remaining sensitive to His guidance, and responding in unwavering agreement.

A consistent immersion in the study and meditation of Scripture becomes a transformative practice, allowing the cleansing power of His word to detoxify us from toxic views and beliefs. The key to this process is a readiness to repent (change our mind) and embrace God's perspective. This is coupled with conscious choices to align our thoughts and attitudes with His timeless truth while actively rejecting or interrupting erroneous thoughts as they emerge, nipping them in the bud before they take root.

## THE POWER OF OUR WORDS

When examining the pivotal role our thoughts and mindsets play in shaping our destinies, it would be incomplete to not address the equally significant role of our words. If we envision our beliefs and mindsets as the engine of a car that direct our decisions and, consequently, our life (sometimes on autopilot, unbeknownst to our consciousness), then our words and tongues serve as the steering wheel.

> Our articulated words, spoken with conviction rather than randomly, act as a direct extension and reflection of our mindsets, offering insight into our thought lives.

The words we utter carry immense power. Our articulated words, spoken with conviction rather than randomly, act as a direct extension and reflection of our mindsets, offering insight into our thought lives. Whether consciously or unconsciously, our speech unveils our deeply rooted beliefs, including attitudes, convictions, and perspectives. Essentially, these are the things we have been pondering and meditating on. As they say, to truly know what someone thinks or believes, one need only pay close attention to their words, for it is through their expressions that their authentic selves are revealed.

Words possess an inherent creative power, as evidenced by God's act of creating the heavens and the earth through His spoken word. As beings made in God's image and likeness, our words, akin to His, carry the potential for creation. Proverbs 18:21 (AMP) emphasizes this power when revealing, "Death and life are in the power of the tongue, and those who love it and indulge it will eat its fruit and bear the consequences of their words."

Our words possess the profound ability to shape our future and destiny, whether for good or bad. Scripture employs a vivid analogy, comparing the relationship between a ship and its rudder to that of the tongue and the entire body. James 3:4-6 (NIV, emphasis added) illustrates this connection:

> "...take ships as an example. Although they are so large and are driven by strong winds, they are steered by a very small rudder wherever the pilot wants to go. Likewise, the tongue is a small part of the body, but it makes great boasts. Consider what a great forest is set on fire by a small spark. The tongue also is a fire, a world of evil among the parts of the body. **It corrupts the whole body, sets the whole course of one's life on fire,** and is itself set on fire by hell."

This Scripture draws attention to the profound impact our words have on our actions, well-being, and the very trajectory of our lives.

Beware! This is not some "name it and claim it" strategy. It is not about declaring whatever we desire in life in an attempt to will it into existence solely through our words and determination.

Rather, it is about learning to control our speech and partnering with God to align our words with His words and promises. It involves connecting and anchoring our faith to His words and confessing His truth over our lives and circumstances. Faith is the force behind our aligned words, setting things into motion. Words spoken without faith do not produce the desired results. Without faith, our words remain mere noise, devoid of fruit.

This coincides with the spiritual law or principle of cause and effect, which God established when He shaped the universe through the power of His spoken words. We see the same law of confession at work during salvation when we believe Christ (and His work on the cross) in our hearts first and confess it with our words. As Romans 10:9-10 (AMP) states,

> "If you declare with your mouth, 'Jesus is Lord,' and believe in your heart that God raised him from the dead, you will be saved. For it is with your heart that you believe and are justified, and it is with your mouth that you profess your faith and are saved."

This principle extends to every area of our lives. What we confess and declare over our lives holds significant weight.

Hence, we have been entrusted with a potent weapon—the power of words. Let us gain the wisdom to use them for our benefit, not to our detriment. May we learn to build with our words and not destroy with them. Let us align ourselves with the wise who are mature enough to "guard their mouths and their tongues [and] keep themselves from calamity" (Proverbs 21:23, NIV).

Finally, it is crucial that we speak God's *rhema* word—His spoken word for the present moment (the now). God communicates His intentions and plans through His fresh and revealed word, which represents His will for our current situations. We cannot presumably choose any Scripture and speak it over our circumstances, expecting that He will bring it to pass according to our timeline and preferences. When we are attuned to His voice, He unveils His will and promises. It is that partnership with His *rhema* word, spoken in agreement and faith, that will yield the desired results. When God hears His rhema words spoken in faith, He acts to bring forth the fulfillment and fruition of our lips (Isaiah 55:11).

As we conclude this chapter, I encourage you to ponder on the power of your thoughts and mindsets, recognizing their impact on shaping your behavior and, ultimately, determining the course of your life. Consider the importance of renewing your mind with the transformative power of the gospel by aligning your thoughts with God's truth. It is essential to have a solid understanding of this topic, as it will be the foundation of everything we discuss in the coming chapters.

Before moving on, I invite you to take a quick inventory of your life and identify areas that will benefit from a mind renewal with the help of the Holy Spirit to bring about the transformation you need. In the next chapter, we will dive into practical ways these negative and destructive thought patterns and wrong beliefs can manifest—which is better known as a poverty mindset. If left unchecked, this mindset will be detrimental to ourselves and the influence God wants us to carry into the world.

## CHAPTER 2

# Dissecting a Poverty Mindset

HAVE YOU EVER faced multiple failures in the same area, start-ing to believe that the situation was hopeless and accepting it as the new norm? Or felt powerless to change your circum-stances after several attempts, only to experience repeated losses in that same area? Well, I have!

I once found myself in this situation, feeling helpless and unable to change my circumstances. My ability to trust God and to live in expectancy was dwindling due to all the disap-pointment. I was almost inclined to accept defeat, forgetting my promises from God. That changed when the Holy Spirit illuminated my thought patterns and the lies I had begun to believe, which were keeping me stuck and preventing me from overcoming those obstacles. He started to expose the false beliefs I was agreeing with that were shaping my reality.

He gently reminded me that these beliefs and thought patterns of helplessness and powerlessness were expressions of a poverty mindset. He revealed His truth to me, which I embraced wholeheartedly, replacing all the lies with His truth. As I renewed my mind with the truth, my faith grew, and my situation began to shift.

The truth is: I am *never* without help—God is my ever-present help! Hope is my inheritance in Christ! Even if my circumstances do not unfold as I wish, He is faithful to fulfill His promises in His timing! His ways are always higher than mine, and His rewards and promises far exceed my expectations as I remain in faith. In my moments of weakness, He makes His grace abound to me so that I have sufficiency in all things, at all times. His power within me empowers me to overcome any challenge, for everyone born of God overcomes the world. On the contrary, a poverty mindset removes God from the equation and envisions the circumstance without Him in it.

> **A poverty mindset removes God from the equation and envisions the circumstance without Him in it.**

## A POVERTY MINDSET DEFINED

A poverty mindset, sometimes referred to as a "scarcity mindset," is a strong belief system centered on the idea of lack. It signifies a limited way of thinking akin to small thinking. It is a deprived mentality that people unconsciously develop over time which influences their thought life, attitudes, and decisions—and subsequently manifesting in tangible aspects of their lives.

Typically, this mindset takes root in our early formative years and solidifies during adulthood. Often, it is modeled by parents or other influential figures, such as teachers or pastors. Additionally, life experiences, particularly negative ones, can contribute to the formation of a poverty mindset in our adult lives. The perpetuation of poverty mindsets can be generational as parents inadvertently pass down these learned mindsets and behaviors (through words or actions) to their children, who, in turn, carry them into adulthood until someone breaks the cycle.

It is a mentality that traps us in beliefs of perceived lack, echoing thoughts and sentiments like, "I don't have enough money, time, or resources," or dwelling on perceived inadequacies such as "I am not smart or talented enough." This mindset tends to make statements like "It's impossible," "I can't do it," "I can't give," or "I can't serve." If these thought patterns become our permanent residence, rather than the occasional places we visit, it is a clear indicator that we are operating in a poverty mindset.

> A poverty mindset has the ability to repel wealth: it originates within but shapes our external reality.

A poverty mindset has less to do with the balance in our bank accounts and more with our internal belief systems. Without discrimination, it affects the rich and poor alike. However, the prevalence of a predominant poverty mindset can directly impact the state of our bank accounts and the overall quality of our lives. Remarkably, it has the ability to repel wealth: it originates within but shapes our external reality.

Here is the good news: we no longer have to dwell in this place! As believers, we are not only called but also empowered to transform our negative and deprived mindsets into positive and godly belief systems. Specifically, we are instructed: "do not be conformed to this world, but be transformed by the renewing of your mind, that you may prove what is that good and acceptable and perfect will of God" (Romans 12:2 NKJV).

Through the enabling power of the Holy Spirit, we have the ability to replace our thought patterns and beliefs with the truth of the gospel, cultivating a mindset that is opposite to a poverty mindset, also known as a "wealth mindset" (a topic we will explore more deeply in the upcoming chapter).

Operating in a wealth mindset is not only far superior but also immensely rewarding compared to living in a poverty mindset. At its core, this mindset embodies qualities such as generosity, gratitude, and contentment. It trusts in God and is anxious for nothing but delights in Him. Regardless of external circumstances, it lives in a consistent state of peace, rest, and joy. Those with a wealth mindset revel in the goodness and love of God, recognizing their earthly existence as an opportunity to be a source of blessing. Rooted in the belief of endless possibilities, they dare to dream big and actively pursue the unique purpose and good works for which they were created (Ephesians 2:10). This mindset rests in the assurance of unlimited resources of heaven and is completely secure, financially, and otherwise. Unlike a poverty mindset, it constantly seeks to be continually extended and grown.

## ARE YOU LACKING IN DREAMS AND VISION?

A significant manifestation of a poverty mindset is the lack of vision for one's life—the inability to dream and dream big. When I speak of dreams, I am not referring to conventional aspirations like owning a big house, driving a fancy car, getting married, or having children. While these are commendable, I am alluding to dreams and visions that transcend personal desires and extend beyond the individual.

I firmly believe that God instills dreams and visions within each of us. We enter this world preloaded and endowed by our Creator. In the words of Sharon Hull, "Dreams are seeds of possibility planted in your soul, calling you to pursue a unique path to the realization of your purpose."[1] We come packed with gifts, talents, and potential deposited into our hearts and innermost beings by God for us to uncover and utilize. This is particularly true for those of us redeemed in Christ who have our spiritual eyes opened and the privilege of hearing His Spirit.

A person with a wealth mindset is attuned to these dreams, dares to discover them, and collaborates with God to bring them to fruition. These God-given dreams and visions are the gateway to fulfilling the good works we are predestined to complete. They are our unique ways and expressions of bringing heaven to earth and advancing the Kingdom of God. Our dreams inherently hold the potential to take us out of financial lack, ushering us into prosperity—God's way of rewarding us for our commitment to pursuing and fulfilling our dreams and visions.

> **Our God-given dreams and visions are the gateway to fulfilling the good works we are predestined to complete. They are our unique ways and expressions of bringing heaven to earth and advancing the Kingdom of God.**

In essence, our dreams and visions are the place of supernatural provision; provision is for the vision. They are the fertile ground where abundance eagerly awaits us. Failing to pursue our dreams and vision is a guaranteed way to miss out on the opportunity for God's abundant blessings. While God provides along the way, especially during the preparation for our destiny, the greatest blessings await those who persevere and reach their destination.

Unfortunately, a person with a poverty mindset forfeits these privileges. This mindset, destructive by nature, robs us of the ability to dream and conceive a vision. It saps our hope for the future, depletes our energy and motivation, and steals our courage. Poverty drains the vitality from our lives, trapping us in a life of survival mode. Without a vision, breaking out of the mold, interrupting the status quo, and venturing into new opportunities and territories becomes difficult. With a poverty mentality, instead of trusting God, fear takes the reins, limiting us from embracing the abundant life that Christ intended for us (John 10:10). A poverty mindset enslaves, harasses, and hides us, preventing us from discovering our true potential in Christ.

## THE MAGNITUDE OF A POVERTY MINDSET

While a poverty mindset originates in the mind, its impact extends beyond mere thoughts. It manifests in the physical realm. Norman Vincent Peale succinctly captures this truth by stating, "Negative thinking definitely attracts negative results."[2] Its destructive influence can reach a broader sphere, affecting various aspects of our lives.

It not only distorts our self-image and our approach to work but also warps our perception of God and others, thereby directly impacting our relationships. A poverty mentality sabotages our destiny, stripping us of the significance and impact we are meant to have within our spheres of influence. Those whom we are destined to serve and impact are deprived of the unique value and blessings we have to offer. In the end, we may leave this world with untapped gifts and unrealized potential, and the world will remain unaware of the fullness of who we were created to be. What a tragedy!

> **A poverty mindset enslaves, harasses, and hides us, preventing us from discovering our true potential in Christ.**

A poverty mindset adds to the complexity because of its potential to permeate successive generations, evolving into a generational curse or stronghold. It transcends individual lives, extending its influence to communities and entire cultures. Unconsciously, generation after generation clings to these ingrained poverty mindsets, accepting distorted and deprived thought patterns as the norm. Breaking free from this cycle becomes a formidable challenge

> A poverty mentality sabotages our destiny, stripping us of the significance and impact we are meant to have within our spheres of influence.

and, even in the presence of positive circumstances, fear driven by these learned mindsets often becomes the dominant force shaping decisions and behaviors.

## BIBLICAL EXAMPLES OF A POVERTY MINDSET

The Bible provides numerous examples of God's people operating out of a poverty mindset. These stories serve as valuable lessons, offering us the chance to learn from their experiences and avoid repeating similar mistakes.

**Example 1:** The first instance unfolds in the book of Genesis when Adam and Eve ate from the tree of the knowledge of good and evil. God had generously granted them everything in the garden, with just one exception of a single tree. They were abundantly provided for in every conceivable way, experiencing no lack. However, Eve (and subsequently Adam) succumbed to deception, entertaining the belief that God was withholding something good from them. By doubting God's goodness and integrity, they allowed greed to enter their hearts, operating from a scarcity mindset. This led them to eat the forbidden fruit, which was forbidden for their own good.

> "For God knows that when you eat from it your eyes will be opened, and you will be like God, knowing good and evil. When the woman saw that the fruit of the tree was good for food and pleasing to the eye, and also desirable for gaining wisdom, she took some and ate it. She also gave some to her husband, who was with her, and he ate it." (Genesis 3:5-6, NIV)

A wealth mindset, on the other hand, trusts in God's love and goodness, acknowledging that He has given us Christ and everything else along with Him. It is anchored in the belief that God will not withhold anything good from us, thereby fostering a deep sense of gratitude for His abundant provision.

**Example 2:** During the Israelites' journey from Egypt to the promised land, God miraculously provided them with supernatural sustenance: the manna in the wilderness. He instructed them to gather only what was needed for the day. Each morning, God covered the ground with an abundance of manna, and everybody had as much as they wanted. However, some Israelites collected more than necessary, motivated by fear and greed stemming from a poverty mindset. Their attempt to save the surplus for the next day resulted in the unfortunate spoilage of the extra food.

> "So Moses told them, 'This is the food the LORD is giving you to eat. The LORD says, "Each of you should gather what you need, a basket of manna for everyone in your family."' So that is what the Israelites did. Some

people gathered a large amount, some people gathered a little. But when they measured what they had gathered, there was no shortage and there was none left over. Everyone gathered just what they needed. Moses told them, 'Don't save that food to eat the next day.' But some of the people did not obey Moses. They saved their food for the next day. But worms got into the food and it began to stink." (Exodus 16:15-20, NIV)

A poverty mindset, characterized by lack of trust in God, is insecure about the future and is fearful of not having enough. This mindset causes a person to look at the world from a scarcity standpoint, operating out of greed and hoarding. In contrast, a wealth mindset trusts in God, understanding the bigger picture of God's generous nature. People with a wealth mindset rest in the abundance of God's economy and not the world's, believing there is more than enough for everybody, even in the wilderness—the difficult seasons. A person with this perspective makes for a good steward of resources.

> **A poverty mindset, characterized by lack of trust in God, is insecure about the future and is fearful of not having enough.**

Example 3: In the wilderness, God instructed Moses to send men to explore Canaan, the promised land He had already declared for the Israelites. Moses selected twelve spies, one from each tribe, to embark on this mission. After forty days of exploration, they returned with their reports. Unfortunately, eight spies provided bad reports (pessimistic accounts), claiming the land was impossible to take over. In contrast, Caleb and Joshua maintained unwavering faith in God's promises.

Despite sharing the same experiences, their perspectives and mindsets greatly differed.

Unfortunately, the Israelites chose to believe the negative report, rejecting God's assurance that the land was already theirs. This lack of belief cost them forty years of aimless, unnecessary wandering in the wilderness. An entire generation, except for a few, perished in unbelief without possessing the promised land. Despite being rescued from slavery in Egypt, they remained slaves in their self-estimation, and their self-perception as "grasshoppers" persisted. This distorted mindset hindered them from realizing their true identity and destiny.

> "But the men who had gone up with him [Caleb] said, 'We can't attack those people; they are stronger than we are.' And they spread among the Israelites a bad report about the land they had explored. They said, 'The land we explored devours those living in it. All the people we saw there are of great size. We saw the Nephilim there (the descendants of Anak come from the Nephilim). **We seemed like grasshoppers in our own eyes, and we looked the same to them.**'" (Numbers 13:31-33, NIV, emphasis added)

A poverty mindset promotes a "grasshopper mentality," marked by an underestimation of oneself and one's abilities—a failure to see and recognize oneself as God does. In contrast, a person with a wealth mindset is "Godfident," perceiving themselves from God's perspective and possessing faith in their giftings and calling. It is crucial not to mistake this elevated self-worth with pride or arrogance, a form of self-confidence that arises when people shape their identity outside of Christ and His potential within them. To the undiscerning eye, they may appear similar externally.

**Example 4:** In the Parable of the Prodigal Son, the youngest son returns home seeking refuge after squandering his inheritance. Overjoyed with his son's return, the father throws him a grand party, lavishing him with good things. He had been saving the fattened calf for such an occasion, and it was time to celebrate. Everyone joins the festivity except the elder brother, who remains angry and resentful in the field.

When the father questions his absence, the older brother responds, "'Look! All these years I've been slaving for you and never disobeyed your orders. Yet you never gave me even a young goat so I could celebrate with my friends'" (Luke 15:29, NIV). Stunned, the father replies, "'You are always with me, and everything I have is yours'" (v. 31).

A poverty mindset is rooted in a servant or slave mentality driven by performance. It tends to be judgmental and susceptible to comparison, lacking an understanding of the Father's grace and goodness. People with this perspective struggle to recognize their status as sons rather than servants, remaining blind to their inheritance in Christ (Galatians 4:7).

## DRIVERS OF A POVERTY MINDSET

While we may all occasionally face a poverty mindset, we have a choice whether to embrace it and make it our permanent home. We have the capacity to change our beliefs and renew our minds. Those who consistently live out of this mindset, rather than visiting it from time to time, exercise their choices to turn it into a constant experience. Many people with a poverty mindset are often unaware and oblivious of its presence in their lives; it is not easily diagnosed!

Nevertheless, it is as much a "mental sickness" as a disease is to the physical body.

Our emotions, particularly the negative ones (like fear, worry, anxiety, and doubt) play a significant role in shaping our beliefs. We often adopt mindsets to nurse certain emotions and, if left unaddressed, they can become a double-edged sword that reinforces a poverty mindset. Repetitive thought patterns likewise generate corresponding emotions, leading to persistent behaviors. For instance, the fear of not having enough money can hinder us from giving financial help to those in need or taking calculated risks in various aspects of life or business. Similarly, individuals trapped in a mindset of lack, convinced they will not have enough, find themselves living in constant fear.

> **A poverty mindset is as much a "mental sickness" as a disease is to the physical body.**

So, how do we discern and become conscious of these detrimental emotions? How can we evaluate them so that they do not influence our thoughts and actions in undesirable ways? Sometimes, these negative emotions become so deeply ingrained that we may not recognize our true selves without them. It is important to note that living with these negative emotions is considered sin in the Bible; they are a distortion of how God originally designed us to function. Consistently operating from these emotions means stepping out of our authentic identity in Christ. Ultimately, our negative emotions stem from a wrong belief (or unbelief) about God, often concerning His love and goodness.

Experiencing negative emotions is normal, albeit briefly. God created emotions, including the negative ones. These negative emotions are only signals in our lives, prompting us to adjust our thinking patterns and refocus on God. We are meant to feel these emotions, use them to our advantage, and then release them. They are not intended to linger and dictate our lives or torment us. They are not meant to be constant companions; they are merely signals! Remember, the Kingdom of God is about righteousness, peace, and joy in the Holy Spirit (Romans 14:17)! Perfect peace, joy, and rest are meant to be our constant companions. Now, let us delve into each of these drivers individually.

## Driver #1: Fear

Fear is a prominent driver (and emotional expression) of a poverty mindset. The Oxford Languages defines fear as "an unpleasant emotion caused by the belief that someone or something is dangerous, likely to cause pain, or a threat."[3] It is synonymous with fright, uneasiness, unrest, nervousness, and panic, representing the opposite of peace, joy, and rest in the soul. For the believer, persistent fear in a specific area often signals a lack of or a diminished trust in God within that realm, indicating an underlying, corresponding incorrect belief, particularly one rooted in a scarcity mindset.

> **The Kingdom of God is about righteousness, peace, and joy in the Holy Spirit! Perfect peace, joy, and rest are meant to be our constant companions.**

Fear manifests in numerous areas, with the most common ones including the fear of death, illness, job or income loss, rejection, and divorce. Fear has a paralyzing effect; it hinders individuals from stepping out and moving forward. Specifically, in the context of a poverty mindset, it manifests as the fear of lack, fear of incompetence (not measuring up), and the fear of not being loved. While the object of fear can vary, its ultimate aim is to confine us to a familiar place or comfort zone, preventing us from stepping out, growing, and fully experiencing abundant life.

Throughout Scripture, God continually encourages, even commands, us not to succumb to fear, emphasizing His constant presence with and in us (see Jeremiah 46:27, Matthew 10:31, and Luke 12:32). Even strong men and women of faith in the Bible occasionally and temporarily experienced fear during challenging times, yet they quickly overcame it by choosing to trust God, relying on His unwavering character and ability. King David eloquently captures this sentiment, declaring, "Even though I walk through the darkest valley, I will fear no evil, for you are with me; your rod and your staff, they comfort me" (Psalm 23:4, NIV). While fleeting moments of fear are inevitable, dwelling on them is not an option.

Fear does not originate from God. His Word affirms that we do not possess the spirit of fear (2 Timothy 1:7). Fear serves as a strategic weapon wielded by the enemy to remove or divert us from God's perfect will, peace, and rest. Fear undermines and weakens our faith and, over time, jeopardizes our destiny—the promised land God has ordained for us. However, as believers, we possess the authority and ability to reject and overcome fear.

### Driver #2: Worry or Anxiety

Worry is another driving factor of a poverty mindset, defined as "giving way to anxiety or unease and allowing one's mind to dwell on difficulty or troubles."[4] It represents a sense of uneasiness about the future that disrupts our peace of mind. Much like fear, worry finds its roots in a lack of trust in God, revealing an underlying link to a corresponding mindset rooted in scarcity.

Distinguishing between concern and worry is crucial. While concern is a healthy response, worry is not. When concern transforms into worry, it indicates a failure to view the challenging situation in light of the sufficiency of Christ. Worrying entails assuming undue responsibility for our lives and the lives of those we care for, even when the situation is beyond our control. Yet, we have a Shepherd whose role is to care for us, regardless of the outcome. The Apostle Peter encourages us: "cast all your anxiety on him because he cares for you" (1 Peter 5:7, NIV).

Worrying signifies a failure to acknowledge that God is greater than any problem we might face and loves us enough to ensure our highest good in every situation. He has our best interests at heart, even when our understanding falls short.

> "'This is why I tell you to never be worried about your life, for all that you need will be provided, such as food, water, clothing—everything your body needs. Isn't there more to your life than a meal? Isn't your body more than clothing?'" (Matthew 6:25, TPT)

### Driver #3: Doubt

Yet another vehicle of a poverty mindset is doubt, defined as "a sense of uncertainty, absence of conviction, or the condition of being double-minded."[5] While doubt can be directed towards oneself or others, in this context, it primarily refers to doubting God.

Doubt presents a unique challenge compared to fear or worry. Being double-minded (or divided) by nature, it can give a false impression that we truly believe something. This is because our believing side can easily mask the unbelieving side, making it more challenging to recognize. Consequently, we may linger in the pit of doubt, prolonging our stay in our current undesirable situation.

"But let him ask in faith, with no doubting, for the one who doubts is like a wave of the sea that is driven and tossed by the wind. For that person must not suppose that he will receive anything from the Lord; he is a double-minded man, unstable in all his ways." (James 1:5-8, ESV)

## SYMPTOMS OF A POVERTY MINDSET

My aim in this section is to open your eyes to potential patterns in your thought process and belief system. Since you have the deepest understanding of yourself, self-diagnosis can be a valuable tool. As you read through the outlined symptoms, I urge you to closely examine yourself. Acknowledging the problem is already half the battle; it marks the initial step towards overcoming it.

Below, you will find an extensive list of symptoms commonly exhibited by a poverty mindset. While not exhaustive, it paints a vivid picture. It is important to note that a person with a poverty mindset regularly exhibits these habits, shaping the fabric of their daily existence. These behaviors are tangible manifestations of the mindset in real-life scenarios. Consider these cues as valuable indicators of whether you predominantly operate from this mindset.

- **Financial Lack.** This stands out as the most visible and quantifiable symptom, indicating a perpetual experience of physical poverty and a scarcity of financial resources. (**Disclaimer:** Not all instances of lack stem from a poverty mindset, as we may all go through seasons of lack in our lives for a reason.) This spectrum ranges from extreme poverty, where the basic necessities of life such as food, shelter, and clothing are lacking, to a continuous struggle to stay afloat, living paycheck to paycheck. For instance, even if you own a house and vehicle(s) but find it challenging to make ends meet consistently, you fall within this category. It is crucial to understand that, by Kingdom standards, having just enough equals experiencing poverty.

- **Inferiority.** This involves the undervaluing of oneself and one's capabilities, similar to the "grasshopper mentality" we previously explored. Typically, low self-esteem takes root in the early years, often arising from a lack of affirmation from authority figures. Additionally, mistreatment or underestimation by others later in life can contribute to this dynamic. Yet, on a profound and elevated level, it is fundamentally a manifestation of not knowing our authentic identity in Christ—a failure to perceive ourselves as God does. (We will dive into the topic of identity in subsequent chapters).

- **Inadequacy.** A close relative of inferiority, inadequacy refers to the state or quality of being insufficient or deficient, leading to a perceived lack of skills or resources. It also encompasses an inability to effectively cope with situations or navigate through life. This mindset *often* expresses itself through statements like, "I can't do," "I can't give," "I can't love," "I can't serve," or "This is impossible."

- **Stinginess.** This is a behavior marked by an unwillingness to give money to those in need. It reflects a reluctance to share time, gifts, and skills with others. When rooted in fear and insecurity of the future, this mindset leads to unfaithfulness and failed stewardship of the resources entrusted to us. Ultimately, it

43

hinders us from experiencing God's blessings and the joy of giving.

- **Ungratefulness.** Consistently carrying a negative attitude and lacking appreciation for the positive aspects of life is considered ungratefulness. It usually stems from being overly focused on problems rather than blessings. When ungratefulness becomes our constant home, we often find ourselves stuck in misery. This disposition creates an atmosphere that repels and drains those around, as opposed to a grateful spirit that produces joy and proves attractive to others.

- **Risk Averseness.** This refers to reluctance to take necessary risks in life, often stemming from a fear of failure and concern about others' opinions if we were to fail. The reluctance to take risks comes at a cost—missed opportunities and unfulfilled dreams and visions. This mindset stands in stark contrast to stepping out in faith; naturally, faith and risk aversion are fundamentally incompatible.

- **Hoarding.** This entails a strong inclination to accumulate possessions as a source of security. A notable expression of this can be the act of saving money for rainy days. Reflecting on this, we should question whether our savings arise from self-sufficiency marked by a lack of trust in God's provision for all seasons of life or wise stewardship fueled by a desire to assign funds for specific plans or projects. Usually driven by fear, hoarding diminishes our capacity to be generous.

- **Small Thinking.** This refers to a limited mindset characterized by an inability to think and dream on a grand scale. Small thinking avoids considering opposing ideas while only relying on similar experiences and people. A person with this mindset has a biased view of the world, shying away from concepts and perspectives that challenge them. This mindset may manifest as an intolerance toward those with differing opinions or experiences, coupled with an inability to step outside their own perspective to understand or empathize with others. It often leads to the formation of rigid, unchangeable opinions on various matters. A person with small thinking differs significantly from an individual with conviction, who actively engages with and considers various perspectives before arriving at a conclusion and remains open to change.

- **Victim Mentality.** As the perfect embodiment of the familiar "poor me" attitude, this mindset habitually attributes problems to others or external sources. Despite acknowledging our ultimate responsibility for our lives and God's sovereignty, this mindset persists in the belief that outside forces control everything that happens to us, leaving us feeling powerless. Even in cases of genuinely being wronged, dwelling in this victimhood perpetuates a poverty mindset.

   In a completely different context, a victim mentality can also manifest as an exclusive reliance on someone external, often God, to experience success or a particular emotional state (e.g., joy). This perspective believes God's help only comes from outside, and it always waits for an external event (something outside of it) to unfold and bring the necessary change. God is not external; He resides within us and is expressed through us (Colossians 1:27). While God does work through others and orchestrates opportunities for us, He primarily works in and through us to bring about the desired changes. We are active participants in His divine Kingdom!

- **Religious Mindset.** Synonymous with a Pharisee spirit, this mindset operates out of a spirit of performance, fueled by effort and striving to earn God's love, favor, and a sense of righteousness. We develop a religious mindset when we fail to understand and rely on His grace. Fundamentally, the religious mindset bases a relationship with God on religious performance rather than acknowledging the transformative work of Jesus on the cross. Any perspective that shifts our focus away from the cross and redirects it to ourselves embodies an essence of self-righteousness.

- **Orphan Mentality.** This mindset comes into play when we lack the knowledge or understanding of our true identity in Christ as children of God. Those with an orphan mentality perceive their relationship with God as a master-slave dynamic, often characterized by a fear of punishment. They view God as distant and demanding, requiring devout pursuit and service. The notions of closeness and intimacy with God are conspicuously absent from their perspective. Their sense of God's love and goodness is conditional on their performance or behavior.

- **Self-Centeredness.** This behavior manifests as the inability to give materially, emotionally, and spiritually to others. Often preoccupied with their own thoughts and feelings, a person with this mindset exhibits a single-minded focus on oneself, prioritizing personal needs, desires, preferences, and problems.

Any giving that does occur is often rooted in a sense of obligation or an expectation of receiving a favor in return. This mindset prioritizes the belief that receiving is superior to giving.

- **Comparison.** Often labeled as the thief of joy, comparison occurs when we struggle with maintaining a healthy self-image, consistently measuring ourselves against others. The root of this mindset lies in our dissatisfaction and lack of contentment with our own identity, possessions, and current circumstances. This tendency emerges when our sense of value and identity is not derived from God and our relationship with Him.

- **Lack of Dreams.** This is the struggle to have grand aspirations or the inability to dream altogether due to the perception that there is insufficient money and resources to accomplish them. This self-imposed limitation takes place when we do not rely on God and His limitless resources. In doing so, we unintentionally limit ourselves and settle for less, overlooking the truth that our God is a God of possibilities (Matthew 19:26).

- **Need for Approval.** This behavior reflects a frequent inclination to seek validation from others, pursuing praise and acceptance when we can find rest in God's unconditional and complete acceptance. A person with this mindset prioritizes being liked and accepted over standing for what is right or truthful, leading them to act out of cowardice. While at times easily noticeable as being "needy," this mindset may also manifest subtly in ways that go unnoticed, often driving high performance and near-perfect behavior to attain approval.

- **Greed.** Usually reflected in the realm of money and power, this behavior involves an insatiable desire for more. This mindset exerts a constant effort to protect one's possessions while taking what rightfully belongs to others. Rooted in the belief that there will never be enough, greed transforms us into takers, often at the expense of others, all in the pursuit of personal security. This greedy mindset creates a false sense of security built on trusting one's financial stability rather than trusting in God's provision and His role as the Source.

- **Envy.** This is an emotion of jealousy that surfaces when witnessing others' success or blessings. Usually, this mindset manifests as an outward display of happiness, a cheerful facade in public, while concealing internal anger and resentment when others succeed. Conversely, it may also represent smiling inwardly and finding secret joy in the failures of others. Yet, those succumbing to envy fail to realize that celebrating others and their success does not diminish the quality of their own lives.

- **Problem-Focused.** This behavior is evident when we choose to fixate and dwell on our challenges—limiting our vision rather than focusing on God's abundance and the unlimited opportunities He provides. This mindset limits our perspective, hindering our ability to recognize and embrace abundance. This tendency arises when we fail to see things from God's perspective and view our circumstances solely through our natural senses (sight and sound), lacking spiritual discernment. It signifies an inability to adopt a viewpoint of victory, established in the finished work of the cross, as opposed to assuming a stand-point of loss or victimhood. While this mind shift can be challenging and requires spiritual maturity, it often leads to a tremendous life transformation.

- **Practicality**. Although beneficial in certain situations, this behavior can serve as a cop-out mechanism and a convenient way of avoiding trust in God. It often masquerades as wisdom, asserting to approach matters realistically while, in reality, viewing them through the lens of unbelief. This mindset frequently resorts to decisions and actions grounded in the observable and tangible rather than in the realm of faith. However, it is crucial to note that anything that does not originate from faith is sin (Romans 14:23). We are called to be a people of faith, understanding that faith is the only way to please God (Hebrews 11:6).

- **Frugality and Thriftiness**. This is a tendency to exercise extreme carefulness in the use of money or resources with the intention of saving money. It celebrates living within scarce means. While living frugally and being thrifty have been highly praised, almost becoming an art (even among Christians), they are expressions of a lack mentality. While being mindful of expenditures and living within one's means is generally commendable, it is important to note that frugality often stems from a fear of scarcity and distrust in God's goodness and provision. This mindset can be mistakenly perceived as prudence or wisdom, with the key distinction found in the underlying motivation, whether rooted in fear or faith.

God created the world for our enjoyment and takes pleasure in providing for us. Living frugally,

however, is offensive to the abundance of the Kingdom and goes against the nature of God. It resembles operating from a beggar mentality rather than
embracing a royalty mindset as a child of the King.

- **Unforgiveness.** This is the decision to withhold
  forgiveness from oneself or others who have caused
  offense while choosing to harbor bitterness in our
  hearts. This mindset is characterized by a reluctance
  to extend mercy to those who may not seem deserv-
  ing. In contrast, God showers us abundantly with
  His mercy and delights in demonstrating it. We can
  even become unforgiving toward ourselves as recipients, showing hesitation to receive God's forgiveness
  and mercy. This reluctance often stems from unbelief
  in God's goodness and gracious nature. This mindset
  may also reveal itself through distancing from God
  and avoiding Him when we feel we have fallen short
  instead of drawing near and allowing Him to transform our minds.

In essence, an awareness of the various manifestations of
a scarcity mindset empowers us to overcome it. Consider this
list a mirror reflecting our mindset through our behaviors.
Its purpose is not to prompt self-fixing or behavioral change
driven by sheer willpower, which is a path disconnected from
grace. Rather, our newfound awareness should lead us to
acknowledgement and repentance—a transformative shift in
our thinking—renewing our minds with the profound truths of
the gospel, which results in an abundance mindset. This shift
in mindset will bring about a transformation in our behaviors.

To bring this chapter to a close, take a moment to reflect on
the key insights and concepts we have covered. From under-

standing the true meaning of a poverty mindset through a Kingdom lens to unraveling the various symptoms it manifests, we have navigated the complexities of living out of a poverty mindset. Fundamentally, this mindset traps us in beliefs of lack and limits our perspectives while infiltrating every aspect of our lives. It enslaves, harasses, and hides us, preventing us from discovering our true identity in Christ and realizing our full potential. It keeps us from entering God's abundance for our lives.

Now that we are equipped with this knowledge, let us journey together in the upcoming chapters on how to break free from this destructive mindset and adopt its superior counterpart: a Kingdom-informed wealth mindset.

# CHAPTER 3

# Demystifying a Wealth Mindset

A FEW YEARS back, I had the privilege of meeting Tracy, an extraordinary woman whose impactful testimony has stayed with me ever since. Her story resonates deeply due to her unwavering trust in God, rooted in her profound wealth mindset.

Tracy and her husband used to own a bed and breakfast, named Pinguin B&B, inspired by her love for penguins. While managing the business, Tracy felt led by God to secure a "1-800" phone number (a common practice at the time), and it became 1-800-PINGUIN. After some time, an insurance company, also named Pinguin, approached her to purchase the number for their business. Initially hesitant, Tracy eventually considered the offer as a means to cover expenses after seeking God's guidance. The company offered a substantial sum, around $10,000, as compensation. Despite the allure of the offer, Tracy felt God urging her to decline.

Though initially perplexed and lacking complete understanding, Tracy chose to trust in God, knowing His character and proven track record in her life. While many small business owners might have succumbed to the temptation to accept the offer to keep their business afloat, Tracy opted to rely on the abundant nature of God and her identity as His cherished daughter.

The representative persistently tried to renegotiate, increasing the offer each time, but Tracy remained steadfast in her decision to decline. Eventually, he informed her that his company was no longer willing to negotiate beyond $20,000. God urged her to stand her ground. Despite doubts creeping in as weeks passed without contact, Tracy held firm, trusting in God's guidance. Then, out of the blue, the representative called one last time with a jaw-dropping offer: $200,000—ten times more than his previous offer. Overwhelmed and speechless, Tracy accepted, knowing it was in alignment with God's will. This extraordinary experience bolstered her confidence in her Father, affirming that God had indeed spoken to her, foretelling that the amount would be akin to a mortgage.

## A WEALTH MINDSET DEFINED

I have often heard the term "wealth mindset" used to describe a set of beliefs, habits, and strategies in investing and wealth-building that distinguishes the financially affluent from others. It is essentially about achieving success and financial prosperity by reshaping one's mental attitude—an interpretation with some validity. However, I believe this definition is overly narrow. A wealth mindset should encompass more than just monetary wealth and riches.

So, what does a wealth mindset entail for Christians? How can we understand it from a Kingdom perspective? Allow me to unpack it using three different angles.

## WEALTH MINDSET: THE MIND OF CHRIST

As I delved into this topic, the Holy Spirit unveiled a profound revelation to me—an insight that *left me in awe*!

From a Kingdom perspective, a wealth mindset embodies the *mind of Christ*—the thoughts, perspectives, and attitudes of God. It refers to how vast, brilliant, abundant, limitless, redemptive, and creative Christ's mind is. For the believer, the mind of Christ is the mind that is controlled by the Holy Spirit (Romans 8:6).

With this new definition, a wealth mindset transcends a limited focus on money or riches, embracing a more holistic and integrated frame of mind. Financial wealth *alone* does not guarantee a wealth mindset! Hence, this understanding of a wealth mindset, rooted in the mind of Christ, offers a comprehensive outlook that applies to every aspect of our lives—our purposes, careers, marriages, relationships, and, yes, our finances.

> From a Kingdom perspective, a wealth mindset embodies *the mind of Christ*—the thoughts, perspectives, and attitudes of God.

Interestingly enough, Scripture tells us that we already possess the mind of Christ: "For who has known the mind and purposes of the Lord, so as to instruct Him? But we have the mind of Christ [to be guided by His thoughts and purposes]." (1 Corinthians 2:16, AMP, emphasis added).

Note that it does not say, "if we have," "we may have," or "we will have." It unequivocally states that we already have it. In other words, it is not a matter of possibility or a future reality; it is a present spiritual truth. Even if we do not fully comprehend or experience it now, this truth remains. And like any other spiritual truth, we possess it by faith first before experiencing it (Hebrews 11:1). We believe first, and then we see. This forms the initial step in renewing our minds: believing that we already have the mind of Christ.

However, what does it truly mean to have the mind of Christ? It signifies having full access to the thoughts, perceptions, and perspectives of Christ Himself. It entails having a thought pattern (mindset), belief system, attitude, and decision-making process that are consistent with the character and nature of Christ. Having the mind of Christ involves viewing situations, people, challenges, money, and life itself through the lens of Jesus' perspective. This represents an excellent and superior way of thinking that is contrary to the mindset prevalent in the world.

At first glance, this appears to be something unreasonable and difficult to fulfill. After all, we are human and not Jesus; how is this possible? It is only possible because we have the Spirit of Christ living in us. The Holy Spirit reveals the wisdom and perspectives of Christ to us.

"The Spirit searches all things, even the deep things of God. For who knows a person's thoughts except their own spirit within them? In the same way, no one knows the thoughts of God except the Spirit of God. What we have received is not the spirit of the world, but the Spirit who is from God, so that we may understand what God has freely given us." (1 Corinthians 2:10-12, NIV)

We have established that the mind of Christ is our new identity, and we are not striving to achieve it but living from the standpoint of already possessing it. However, we still need to grow and mature in our understanding of it until we reach the full measure and stature of Christ. This does not come about by chance or accident; it takes "effort" and intentionality. We have to nurture it. While it is our inherent potential, we must learn to fully engage and utilize it.

Cultivating the mind of Christ requires spending quiet time in the presence of God. Just as spending ample time with someone inevitably leads to adopting their ways of thinking and mannerisms, being in God's presence renews our minds and transforms us into His likeness—aligning our thoughts and ways with His. In this place, our spiritual senses of sight, hearing, touch, smell, and taste are sharpened, enabling us to discern God's thoughts, ways, and purposes. As Hebrews 5:14 (AMP) states: "But solid food is for the [spiritually] mature, whose senses are trained by practice to distinguish between what is morally good and what is evil." Growing and maturing in the mind of Christ entails receiving solid spiritual food from the Source in His presence.

Growing in the mind of Christ also necessitates knowing and understanding His word. The word of God washes over us, cleansing our thinking. Truth renews our minds. As new creations in Christ, even though our inner man is new, our old mindset and its programming must be replaced with the new realities of the Kingdom, enabling us to think from heaven to earth.

## WEALTH MINDSET: ENDLESS POSSIBILITIES

From this perspective, a wealth mindset is defined as one that embraces limitless or unlimited possibilities. This mindset looks beyond the present to what is unfolding. It sees into the realm of possibility—the divine or supernatural realm. It is grounded in the realization that "All things are possible to him who believes!" (Mark 9:23, NIV). It lives and functions in an atmosphere of faith and is full of hope.

A wealth mindset sees opportunity amid challenges, holds onto hope during times of despair and confusion, and envisions possibilities in the midst of the impossible. It carries confidence, peace, and joy in the wilderness, knowing that God is with and in us. The potential of what it can achieve is limitless because it believes "...I can do everything through Christ, who gives me strength" (Philippians 4:13, NLT). This mentality looks beyond its abilities and strength and relies on what God can do. It aligns its thoughts and words with sentiments such as "it is possible," "I can do it," and "I have what it takes."

> A wealth mindset looks beyond the present to what is unfolding. It sees into the realm of possibility—the divine or supernatural realm.

Do not be fooled! People who embody this mindset are not perfect by any means. They will go through their share of discouragement, confusion, and despair. However, they will bounce back to being encouraged and hopeful, knowing that they have a good Father "who is able to [carry out His purpose and] do superabundantly more than all that we dare ask or think [infinitely beyond our greatest prayers, hopes, or dreams], according to His power that is at work within us" (Ephesians 3:20, AMP). Their down moments are few and far between. They will visit these places from time to time but choose to dwell in the realm of faith and possibilities. People with this mindset do not deny the facts on the ground; they simply choose to believe and view their circumstances through the eyes of faith. They believe in the truth more than the facts.

## WEALTH MINDSET: ABUNDANCE AND PROSPERITY

From this angle, a wealth mindset is defined as an abundance or prosperity mindset. *Oops...did I say prosperity?* I know it is sometimes considered a taboo word, but bear with me! We will address the elephant in the room later in this section.

This mindset believes and rests in the truth of God's abundant nature and that there is no lack found in Him. It is rooted in the conviction that Jesus came so we "'may have and enjoy life, and have it in abundance [to the full, till it overflows]'" (John 10:10, AMP). Just as a poverty mindset attracts poverty, a wealth mindset attracts abundance and repels scarcity. Chris Vallotton beautifully sums up this idea:

> **People with a wealth mindset do not deny the facts on the ground; they simply choose to believe and view their circumstances through the eyes of faith. They believe in the truth more than the facts.**

"Wealth is believing in the fullness of God's ability and desire to provide in your life. It's the means—resources, strength, and wisdom—to create positive outcomes in the midst of lack. It is light in the darkness, healing in sickness, prosperity in poverty, wholeness in brokenness, favor in obscurity, love for the unlovely, beauty for ashes, and victory among victims."

Surprisingly, a wealth mindset is not limited to Christians alone. Even the scientific and secular worlds have caught up to this truth. A wealth mindset stands as a universal principle that works for everyone who adopts and practices it. Many millionaires, billionaires, and successful people possess and apply this abundant thinking. While they may not know Christ or have access to His Spirit to discern His thoughts and perceptions, their thinking aligns with an abundance mindset. In fact, I have come across more unbelievers with a wealth mindset than believers. It is a very sad but sobering reality!

One would naturally expect that as people who believe in God (the God of possibilities) and who are connected to the Source—life, wisdom, knowledge, resources, and much more—we would excel at this mindset. So why are believers lacking in this mindset? Why has the world surpassed us in embracing and embodying this abundant mindset? I believe there are three key reasons:

1. We don't *fully* know and understand who our God is—His nature.
2. We don't *fully* understand who we are—our identity in Christ.
3. We don't *fully* understand the enemy's tactics— deception and confusion.

The first two reasons will be discussed at length in the following chapters. However, for now, I would like to focus on the last reason: the enemy's schemes to rob us of an abundance mindset.

## EXPOSING THE ENEMY'S TACTICS

Since the beginning, Satan's plan has been to separate us from God, obstructing our understanding of His goodness, love, and magnificent plan for us. Unfortunately, we have succumbed to his deceitful narratives, embracing a mindset of scarcity. Deceived, we live outside God's will of abundance and prosperity. It is no wonder the Bible refers to him as the father of lies (John 8:44).

Nevertheless, if we understand the truth, it will liberate us (John 8:32). We can only recognize the counterfeit by becoming acquainted with the authentic. Let's break down the primary ways the devil has deceived us, diverting us from a life of God's abundance.

## 1. Corruption

On this extreme end, the enemy deceives us into believing that we can live by the same standards as the world. We resort to lies, deception, cheating, and shortcuts. We wear ourselves out in the pursuit of wealth through corruption or any means possible rather than working with integrity. Greed takes hold of us, driving us to do whatever it takes to get ahead. It mirrors the behavior of the world, which the Bible refers to as "ill-gotten gain" (Proverbs 10:2).

Such wealth does not originate from God and fails to bring blessings to us (Proverbs 10:22). In the long term, it does not lead to a life of abundance, financially or otherwise. In fact, it often leads to disaster. Scripture, specifically the Proverbs, clearly speaks of the consequences of corrupt behavior sooner or later:

"Treasures gained by wickedness do not profit, but righteousness delivers from death." (Proverbs 10:2, ESV)

"Such are the ways of everyone who is greedy for unjust gain; it takes away the life of its possessors." (1:19)

"Whoever is greedy for unjust gain troubles his own household, but he who hates bribes will live." (15:27)

## 2. Performance and Striving

Unfortunately, common among many Christians, this tactic of the enemy is very subtle and disguises itself as "good," only perpetuating religion. This kind of deception primarily manifests in two ways:

A. *When we strive to earn God's love and favor for provision and abundance through our efforts and willpower rather than through grace.* Provision and prosperity are our inheritance in Christ as we seek Him first. We receive them as free gifts through faith as beloved children of God. We do not have to perform *for* God to earn these benefits; doing so disconnects us from grace and from freely receiving these blessings. This could take the form of praying long and hard, serving in the church, reading the Bible, or doing good works—all wonderful disciplines when done out of a desire for intimacy with God and not out of expectation for repayment (often secretly or subconsciously) from God.

B. *When we solely rely on our wisdom, smarts, and skills rather than trust God and depend on Him for our provision.* This is when we forget that God is the giver and sustainer of all things, including our intelligence, gifts, and capabilities. We may say to ourselves, "'My power and the strength of my hands have produced this wealth for me.' But remember the Lord your God, for it is he who gives you the ability to produce wealth" (Deuteronomy 8:17-19, NIV). God is well pleased when we employ our gifts and abilities for good work, keeping our eyes on the Source and acknowledging our dependence on Him for all things.

Trusting and depending on God for provision does not negate, and by no means diminishes, the value of excellent work and diligence. God often blesses us through the work of our hands. I am simply emphasizing that self-sufficiency (the attempt to earn grace) and self-dependence are the culprits that block God's abundance. Performance and striving disconnect us from His grace.

### 3. Distortion

Another effective scheme the enemy employs to deceive us, particularly in recent church history, is distorting the truth about biblical abundance and prosperity. One such tactic is through the introduction of the prosperity gospel, a teaching that has confused, misguided, and misled many believers into strongly pursuing money and riches without pursuing God Himself. Many have been bewitched with "get rich quick" schemes and teachings, causing them to move their focus away from the main prize—Christ.

> In the Kingdom's order of importance, intimacy with God takes precedence ... Everything else flows from that intimacy.

As always, the enemy takes what is true in God's word and twists it to make it palatable for many. In the case of the prosperity gospel, he creates a misplaced priority and reverses the order of importance of Kingdom values.

In the Kingdom's order of importance, intimacy with God takes precedence. First things first! Everything else flows from that intimacy. A heart that is well aligned with God's heart is well positioned to receive from Him, stewarding His provisions and blessings well without any misuse or abuse of what has been given.

> "But first and **most importantly** seek (aim at, strive after) His kingdom and His righteousness [His way of doing and being right—the attitude and character of God], and **all these things** will be given to you also." (Matthew 6:33, AMP, emphasis added)

Are we regularly seeking His hands more than His face? Are we consistently pursuing the blessings or the giver Himself? It is time to recalibrate!

## 4. A Religious Spirit

When it comes to abundance and prosperity, the religious spirit can manifest in various forms, often revealing itself through extreme teachings and convictions. On one end of the deception spectrum, there is corruption, performance, and the prosperity gospel. On the other side, we have the "poverty gospel"—a belief system that equates poverty with holiness and godliness while promoting wealth and prosperity as sinful or evil. Essentially, it suggests that holiness and prosperity cannot coexist.

In various Christian backgrounds, individuals have relinquished the notion of personal ownership of property as part of a religious commitment that has influenced their perspectives on wealth and prosperity. Advocates of the poverty gospel often cite, "Blessed are the poor in spirit, for theirs is the kingdom of heaven" (Matthew 5:3, ESV). However, what does being "poor in spirit" truly entail? Jesus was referring to those who are spiritually bankrupt but humbly admit their inability to earn salvation, those who acknowledge their need for a savior.

While the poverty gospel has long been present, I believe the rise of the prosperity gospel has driven many to this edge. I sense that in their fervent rejection of the prosperity gospel and its teachings, many Christians swung to the opposite extreme and altogether dismissed biblical prosperity and abundance. Many discarded what was sacred and pure, along with the impurities and lies. As the old saying goes, they "threw out the baby with the bathwater." It may serve us well to differentiate between prosperity and materialism, the latter being the persistent drive to define our identities based on both our current possessions and those we aspire to possess in the future.

In my view, Satan has inflicted more damage to the church through the poverty gospel than the prosperity gospel. This belief system has not just robbed us of God's abundance and provision but also incurred an opportunity cost—the missed opportunities to build and advance the Kingdom.

## BIBLICAL TRUTH ABOUT PROSPERITY

It is disheartening to witness how prosperity has turned into a taboo word in many churches. Many Christians are conditioned to immediately reject it and put up their guard and defenses when they hear the word. Some automatically label it as false teaching without seeking understanding. How do I know? Because I was once among them! However, God began to teach me what biblical prosperity truly is and how to distinguish and decipher the various teachings surrounding it. Given that the word "prosperity" is often used in reference to wealth or money, it might be worth focusing on what biblical prosperity entails.

> A prosperous spirit is ever-increasing and thriving, experiencing the inner life of God. A prosperous soul includes a prosperous mind, one that is renewed by the truth of the gospel . . . A prosperous body enjoys good health, success, and fruitfulness in all its endeavors.

The term "prosperity" is a holistic and comprehensive concept that encompasses spirit, soul (mind and emotions), and body—not solely limited to financial wealth. The Apostle John, in his letter to a fellow believer, writes, "Beloved, I pray that you may prosper in all things and be in health, just as your soul prospers" (3 John 1:2, NKJV), indicating that prosperity is an all-encompassing notion. Our spirit—inner man—is inherently perfect and prosperous as it is born from above (born of the Spirit). It remains prosperous as it is continuously replenished, strengthened, and nourished by the Holy Spirit and the word of God. A prosperous spirit is ever-increasing and thriving, experiencing the inner life of God.

A *prosperous soul* includes a prosperous mind, one that is renewed by the truth of the gospel. It is aligned and consistent with the mind of Christ, reflecting a mindset of wealth. A prosperous soul also encompasses a prosperous emotional life—emotional wholeness and well-being—fostering an inner environment grounded in the Kingdom culture of perfect peace, indescribable joy, and deep fulfillment in God.

A *prosperous body* enjoys good health, success, and fruitfulness in all its endeavors. Physical prosperity extends to healthy relationships and financial well-being (stability), embodying completeness in all areas and lacking nothing.

Additionally, examining the Hebrew and Greek root words for "prosperity" provides a richer insight into the essence of the term. A Blue Letter Bible LexiConc search for the word "prosper" in the King James Bible yields the following results. You will notice that the English equivalents of the transliterated Hebrew and Greek words, which can also be considered synonyms of prosperity, encapsulate completeness in every aspect of life. They range from emotional wellness (depicted as happiness, peace, and quietness) to gaining skill, understanding, wisdom, and achieving success, wealth, and abundance.

Demystifying a Wealth Mindset

*Figure 1. Blue Letter Bible: Strong's Concordance Hebrew and Greek Transliterations for "Prosper"* [1]

| Strongs # | Hebrew | Transliterated | English Equivalent |
|---|---|---|---|
| H2896 | טוֹב | ṭôḇ | good, better, well, goodness, goodly, best, merry, fair, **prosperity**, precious, fine, wealth, beautiful, fairer, favor, glad, misc |
| H3787 | כָּשֵׁר | kāšēr | right, **prosper**, direct |
| H6743 | צָלַח | ṣālēaḥ | **prosper**, come, **prosperous**, come mightily, effected, good, meet, break out, went over, misc |
| H6744 | צְלַח | ṣᵊlaḥ | **prosper**, promote |
| H7919 | שָׂכַל | śāḵal | understand, wise, **prosper**, wisely, understanding, consider, instruct, prudent, skill, teach, misc |
| H7951 | שָׁלָה | šālâ | **prosper**, safety, happy |
| H7959 | שֶׁלֶו | šelev | **prosperity** |
| H7961 | שָׁלֵו | šālēv | at ease, peaceable, quietness, **prosperity**, quiet, **prosper**, wealthy |
| H7962 | שַׁלְוָה | šalvâ | **prosperity**, peaceably, quietness, abundance, peace |
| H7965 | שָׁלוֹם | šālôm | peace, well, peaceably, welfare, salute, **prosperity**, did, safe, health, peaceable, misc |
| Strongs # | Greek | Transliterated | English Equivalent |
| G2137 | εὐοδόω | euodoō | **prosper**, have a **prosperous** journey |

Hence, if wholeness is God's best for us, why would we settle for anything less? These may seem unrealistic or out of touch to some, but Jesus already paid for them on the cross. Through faith and perseverance, we can inherit them.

Another misconception is that many Christians think pros-

67

perity is a new concept or teaching. However, it is as old as God Himself—the God of all ages. It was not recently introduced by New Agers or prosperity gospel preachers. All throughout Scripture, God's abundance and prosperity permeate. It is extensively covered in both the Old and New Testaments. Particularly in the Old Testament, the essence of prosperity was intricately woven into the lives of the Israelites. It was built into the covenants God made with Abraham and the other forefathers. This is how God interacted and dealt with His people, how He chose to bless them through His many promises, especially as a reward for observing the laws.

If the old covenant, based on rules and regulations, was abundant with God's promises to prosper the Israelites, how much more would the new covenant, founded on grace and far superior to the old, offer prosperity to us who believe in Christ? For we know, "the ministry Jesus has received is as superior to theirs [high-priests] as the covenant of which he is mediator is superior to the old one, **since the new covenant is established on better promises**" (Hebrews 8:6, NIV, emphasis added).

In this new covenant of grace, we are not required to perform or uphold the law to receive His abundance. Instead, we possess it by faith through the *finished* work of the cross (John 10:10). It is one of the many benefits (promises) of the gospel. Those who persevere in faith and do not give up will inherit His promises. Surely, the spiritual "violent" take their inheritance in Christ, their promises, by force (Matthew 11:12). While God's promises are yes and amen in Christ, it does not mean they come easily or without a fight. This is the fight of faith. Faith does not make things easy; it makes them possible! After all, perseverance produces the necessary character in us to carry and steward His abundance well.

## BIBLICAL EXAMPLES OF A WEALTH MINDSET

The Bible recounts the stories of men and women of faith who lived out of a wealth mindset, viewing their circumstances through God's perspective of abundance.

**Example 1:** In contrast to the poverty mindset of the ten spies in the previous chapter, let's turn our attention to the two individuals with a wealth mindset: Caleb and Joshua. They were among the twelve spies representing the tribes of Judah and Ephraim, whom Moses sent to scout the land of Canaan. After surveying the land, the other ten spies delivered a unanimous negative report to Moses, Aaron, and the Israelites:

> "The land through which we have gone as spies is a land that devours its inhabitants, and all the people whom we saw in it are men of great stature. There we saw the giants (the descendants of Anak came from the giants); and we were like grasshoppers in our own sight, and so we were in their sight." (Numbers 13:32-3,3 NKJV).

However, Joshua and Caleb presented a different report:

> The land through which we passed as spies is an exceedingly good land. If the Lord delights in us, then He will bring us into this land and give it to us, a land which flows with milk and honey. Only do not rebel against the Lord; and do not fear the people of the land, for they will be our prey. Their protection has been removed from them, and the Lord is with us. Do not fear them. (Numbers 14:7-9, AMP)

"Let us go up at once and take possession of it; for we will certainly conquer it." (Numbers 13; 30, AMP)

All twelve spies observed the same aspects in Canaan, yet Joshua and Caleb had a different mindset—one that viewed difficult circumstances from God's perspective. It is no wonder that God Himself boasts about Caleb: "'But my servant Caleb has a different attitude than the others have. He has remained loyal to me, so I will bring him into the land he explored. His descendants will possess their full share of that land,'" (Numbers 14:24, NLT). Caleb chose to trust God and His promise, being confident in His character and ability. His focus remained on God and His greatness rather than the giants in the land. Consequently, Caleb and Joshua were the only ones from that generation of Israelites who possessed the land and inherited God's promise.

> **A wealth mindset is not content with the average or ordinary; instead, it aspires toward higher and better things.**

**Example 2:** The prophet Ezekiel is brought to a valley filled with dry bones by the Spirit of the Lord, a situation that seems hopeless and filled with despair. God asks Ezekiel if these bones can live, and Ezekiel responds, "'Sovereign Lord, you alone know'" (Ezekiel 37:3, NIV), making room for God's possibilities. Then God instructs Ezekiel to prophesy to the dry bones and bring them to life. As he prophesied over the dry bones, they transformed into a vast army.

Ezekiel was given a seemingly impossible task, one he could easily deem unrealistic and feel unqualified to complete. Yet, Ezekiel did not respond with "No, it is impossible!", nor did he throw out excuses for his inability and inadequacy. Because he possessed a wealth mindset, he simply trusted God and obliged. He knew that God was a God of possibilities. He understood that God's instructions and assignments contained within them the power to make one fully capable and qualified.

## SYMPTOMS OF A WEALTH MINDSET

Below, you will find an extensive (though not exhaustive), list of symptoms that are indicative of a wealth mindset. This resource will help you assess your mindsets in light of your understanding of God's abundant nature. Should you identify with these attributes and notice their frequent presence in your life, it is possible you are operating from a wealth mindset. These traits typically contrast with those of a poverty mindset.

> A wealth mindset does not solely live for the here and now; it aims to make a meaningful impact and leave a lasting legacy.

Remember, these attributes reflect your potential in Christ, and there is always room for growth and transformation.

- **Purpose or Vision.** Do you have a sense of purpose in your life? Do you have a vision bigger than yourself or your family? Even better, are you pursuing it? If so, these are positive indicators that you might possess an abundance mindset. A wealth mindset is not content with the average or ordinary; instead, it aspires toward higher and better things. It does not view money as an end in itself—simply accumulating materials or riches—but rather as a means (tool) to fulfill its vision or purpose. For those with a wealth mindset, money is a by-product and a reward for pursuing and accomplishing their God-given visions.

This mindset does not solely live for the here and now; it aims to make a meaningful impact and leave a lasting legacy.

- **Ability to Dream.** Do you find yourself dreaming regularly? And when you dream, do you dream big? This inclination is a healthy sign of a wealth mindset. Not only do those with this mindset dream, but they also actively pursue those dreams. Their aspirations transcend self-interest and selfish ambition, reaching for objectives larger than the individual. They aspire for improvement and are not hindered by resource limitations when it comes to dreaming because they know the Source.

- **Risk-Taking.** If those with a wealth mindset dare to dream, they also dare to take risks. They are not held back by the fear of failure or disapproval. Past setbacks and rejections do not define them. Should a failure occur, they pick themselves up and move on or persevere, understanding that failure is integral to the learning and growth process. They disregard the voices of pessimists and naysayers. They acknowledge that taking risks costs something but also recognize that playing it safe costs much more.

- **Gratitude.** A wealth mindset has cultivated the practice of gratitude, and those who have it consistently express thanks for the many blessings from God, particularly for what Jesus has accomplished on the cross. This mindset focuses on what it already possesses rather than what it lacks. It accentuates the positive aspects of life instead of dwelling on the negative, maximizing its strengths rather than fixating on weaknesses.

- **Generosity.** Unfettered by fear of lack, individuals with a wealth mindset have developed the capacity to give—materially, emotionally, and spiritually. They give freely out of genuine desire and joy, not out of obligation or guilt, understanding that giving is more fulfilling than receiving. Grounded in the knowledge of their Source, they feel no compulsion to hoard or cling to possessions. This mindset derives satisfaction from meeting needs and doing good in the world, motivated by a compassionate heart for the poor and oppressed.

> Individuals with a wealth mindset live in the realm of faith, daring to think and believe big, embracing endless possibilities.

- **Hopeful.** A wealth mindset is hopeful about the future and lives with a sense of anticipation and expectancy. Even in the face of adversity, individuals with this mindset remain hopeful and optimistic, understanding the redemptive nature of God. Instead of seeing problems in opportunities, they seek out and capitalize on opportunities within challenges. They firmly believe in possibilities and take responsibility for situations—initiating action rather than resorting to blame or complaint. This mindset focuses on God's promises rather than on potential negative outcomes, maintaining a positive outlook on life.

- **Trusting.** Individuals with a wealth mindset believe in the goodness of God and His desire and ability to provide for them. Rooted in trust, they do not succumb to fear or worry about lack. They are secure about the future, resting in the knowledge that God is their ultimate Source. Embracing a childlike faith, they exude confidence in the Father's faithfulness to abundantly provide for His children. They live in the realm of faith, daring to think and believe big, embracing endless possibilities.

- **Child-of-God Mentality.** A wealth mindset finds security in its identity as a beloved child of God. In contrast to an orphan mentality, its perception of God is characterized by goodness, love, and grace. It recognizes and embraces being loved, accepted, and favored. Those marked by this mindset hold the highest priority of cultivating a relationship with God rather than rigid adherence to rules and regulations. Understanding that service is born out of a place of love and not obligation or fear of displeasing God, they prioritize intimacy over mere service. Individuals with a wealth mindset become "lovers of God," actively demonstrating their love through their actions and outworking duty-bound "workers for God."

- **Confident (Godfident).** A wealth mindset derives its confidence from knowing its identity in Christ. Its confidence radiates through its disposition, speech, and actions, which may occasionally be misconstrued as cocky or arrogant by others. Secure in itself, it is not inclined to compare itself with others. It embraces authenticity over imitation of others, rejecting the pressure to conform to societal standards or "keeping up with the Joneses." Unswayed by external opinions, these individuals remain steadfast in their convictions. They do not live to please others or seek approval; rather, they acknowledge an audience of one.

- **Celebrates Others.** Individuals with a wealth mindset find genuine happiness in the success of others, understanding that their wins and accomplishments do not mean their loss. They are not envious when others do well; instead, they celebrate it. Witnessing the significant triumphs of others serves as motivation, inspiring them to strive for improvement and set loftier goals.

- **Mindful.** A wealth mindset understands the power of its thoughts and words. It remains conscious of the dominant thoughts circulating in its mind and the words spoken, recognizing their power to shape both the present and, significantly, the future. Deliberately choosing its thoughts and words wisely and making sure they align with the truths of the gospel, it endeavors to create an abundant life and a better future.

> Secure in itself, a wealth mindset is not inclined to compare itself with others. It embraces authenticity over imitation of others, rejecting the pressure to conform to societal standards.

- **Good Company.** Individuals with a wealth mindset intentionally surround themselves with those who are like-minded—those who aspire to learn and grow, have dreams and visions, embody honesty, and are committed to launching others into their destiny. Echoing the sentiments of Warren Buffet, who is quoted as saying, "Surround yourself with people that push you to do better. No drama or negativity. Just higher goals and higher motivation. Good times and positive energy. No jealousy or hate. Simply bringing out the absolute best in each other."

This mindset desires to be in thriving environments with people who inspire, challenge, enlighten, encourage, and support others. It does not waste *significant* time in the company of individuals who consistently exhibit pessimism, disgruntlement, and criticism toward others. As Mark Twain wisely advises, "Keep away from people who try to belittle your ambitions. Small people always do that, but the really great make you feel that you, too, can become great."[2] Importantly, this principle does not conflict with serving and loving others in their times of need.

- **Quality.** Individuals with a wealth mindset appreciate quality in all aspects of life. They believe that they are worthy of good things because of the worthiness God ascribes to them in Christ Jesus. Recognizing their royal status as sons of the Most High King, they direct their resources, time, and money toward what exemplifies "quality"—whether in time spent, experiences had, relationships fostered, food savored, education pursued, business ventures undertaken, financial investments made, and more. They take pleasure in excellent work and relish the rewards of their labor. Embracing the essence of a quality life, they remain open to new ideas, experiences, people, and cultures. They revel in exploring life's wonders, creating adventures and memories, while also finding solace in relaxation and enjoyment.

- **Merciful.** Individuals with a wealth mindset understand from experience that God is faithful to forgive and abundant in mercy. They are willing to extend this abundant mercy to themselves and others, even when it hurts. They have learned the importance of continuously cleansing their hearts through forgiveness, as they are fully convinced that goodness flows only from a healed heart, in alignment with the wisdom in Proverbs 4:23: "Keep your heart with all diligence, For out of it spring the issues of life" (NKJV).

As we close this chapter, we have explored how to rethink and define a wealth mindset from a Kingdom perspective. Specifically, we first noted that possessing a wealth mindset equates to having the mind of Christ—having access to His thoughts, perceptions, and perspectives—which qualifies us to view the world through His eyes. Secondly, we discussed how a wealth mindset is anchored in possibilities, rejecting beliefs of limitations and embracing God's endless possibilities to interpret our circumstances. Eventually, we settled that a wealth mindset is fully aware and convinced of the prosperous and abundant nature of God, enabling us to view all things not through the lens of lack, but through abundance.

> **Individuals with a wealth mindset believe that they are worthy of good things because of the worthiness God ascribes to them in Christ Jesus.**

In the upcoming chapters, under the part *Renewal*, we will discuss the process of cultivating this exceptional mindset by renewing our minds with foundational truths. Simply awakening to these truths and embracing them constitutes a significant part of the work required to cultivate a wealth mindset. Let us begin this next chapter by immersing ourselves in the truth of the gospel, a foundation that will help reframe our thinking and beliefs as we adopt a wealth mindset.

# PART 2

# RENEWAL

———

## CHAPTER 4

# The Gospel Unveiled

UNDERSTANDING THE GOSPEL is fundamental in every aspect, but it holds a particularly foundational role in cultivating a wealth mindset. Essentially, renewing our minds with the truths of the gospel lays the groundwork for abundant thinking in the Kingdom. This process is vital to forming eyes of faith, which allow us to perceive the world from God's perspective rather than solely through our natural senses.

If you are reading this book, chances are you are a born-again believer. Upon seeing the title of this chapter, you may wonder why there is a need to revisit your understanding of the gospel. I understand your perspective! You may feel like I am preaching to the choir, but first, allow me to explain.

You see, many of us, myself included, were not taught the gospel correctly. Despite being a born-again and Spirit-filled Christian for several years, deeply valuing my relationship with God, and possessing a solid understanding of Scripture, I was surprised when the gospel pleasantly hit me in the face like a revelation. It was the first time in my Christian walk that the gospel of Jesus Christ truly came to life for me, completely turning my world upside down. I found myself asking, both to myself and others, "Why was I never taught this before?" I felt frustration toward the church for failing to impart this knowledge to me earlier. I was also disappointed with the numerous teachers and preachers I encountered along the way. However, as my anger subsided, I realized that they could not teach me what they themselves did not know.

For the first time, I truly understood why it is called the Good News! The original version of the gospel, without any mix of religion, was incredibly good—perhaps even too good to be true! No wonder it spread like wildfire in the early church. It was the first time I felt genuinely excited to preach the gospel; it was no longer a burden or a duty as a Christian. I could not keep my mouth shut—I was even preaching it to myself (which I highly recommend, by the way). Even after many years, it still burns afresh in my heart. The gospel is all too magnificent, irresistible, and exhilarating!

> **The gospel is all too magnificent, irresistible, and exhilarating!**

## COMMON MISUNDERSTANDINGS OF THE GOSPEL

If you are not excited about the gospel, perhaps it is time to rediscover this wonderful news! Receiving a revelation of the gospel has the power to transform your life from the inside out (Sometimes, this revelation is something you catch rather than something you learn). Once we receive it, it will start to free us from all the religious bondages we may not even realize we are carrying. It will wash away any distorted thinking or beliefs we have held as a result of the sin in the world, which causes separation from God in our minds.

Here are some major misunderstandings of the gospel.

Firstly, we have been taught about the gospel (or the cross) as if it is merely the entry point to Christianity—the means or the introduction through which we were brought into the Christian faith. And to some extent, this is true. However, the gospel is not just the entry point or a doorway. We do not simply pass through it and leave it behind. It is the exciting beginning, the delightful middle, and the glorious end. It is the every-day reality for eternity. It is the oxygen that gives us life and sustains us indefinitely.

> The gospel is not just the entry point or a doorway . . . It is the exciting beginning, the delightful middle, and the glorious end.

Secondly, we have been taught that the gospel is elementary—as if it is something basic that we start with but then move on to bigger and better things. This could not be further from the truth! The gospel is the basic, the intermediate, and the advanced all at once. It is the cornerstone, the columns, the roof, and everything in between. It is the solid foundation from which we begin and upon which we build. It is also the lens through which we study and interpret all of Scripture—both the Old and New Testaments. This lens reveals and magnifies Christ, the Living Word, on every page of the Bible. The gospel stands as the ultimate truth, which we continually grow in revelation and understanding.

The Apostle Paul, with all his learning and understanding of Scripture, was consumed with the gospel. Above all else, he resolved to know Christ and Christ alone—the epicenter of the gospel. He says,

"**For I made the decision to know nothing** [that is, to forego philosophical or theological discussions regarding inconsequential things and opinions while] among you

except Jesus Christ, and Him crucified [and the meaning
of His redemptive, substitutionary death and His resurrection." (1 Corinthians 2:2, AMP, emphasis added).

If Paul made it his life's mission to know this one thing
alone, I believe we should follow suit. You see, the gospel is a
mystery—the hidden wisdom of Christ that is unveiled, layer
by layer, right before our eyes daily through the Holy Spirit (1
Corinthians 2:6-7). Oh, the breadth and the depth of the cross!

Thirdly, many Christians are taught the gospel as a mix of
grace and law. However, in the equation of the gospel, there
is only grace, as grace plus law always equals law. Many
born-again believers still find
themselves with one foot in
the new covenant of grace and
the other foot in the covenant
of the law (governed by rules
and regulations). While they
begin in grace for their salvation, they unknowingly shift
towards self-effort and performance. They adopt a do-it-your-
self perspective to maintain their salvation, which ultimately
disconnects them from grace.

> The gospel is a mystery—the
> hidden wisdom of Christ that
> is unveiled, layer by layer,
> right before our eyes daily
> through the Holy Spirit.

The Apostle Paul warned the Galatians against such ten-
dencies when they attempted to add one more self-righteous
act, circumcision, to their salvation. He questioned:

"You foolish Galatians! Who has bewitched you? Before
your very eyes Jesus Christ was clearly portrayed as
crucified. I would like to learn just one thing from you:
Did you receive the Spirit by the works of the law, or
by believing what you heard? Are you so foolish? After

beginning by means of the Spirit, are you now trying to finish by means of the flesh? Have you experienced so much in vain—if it really was in vain? So again I ask, does God give you his Spirit and work miracles among you by the works of the law, or by your believing what you heard?" (Galatians 3:1-5, NIV)

The message of the cross is "done," while the message of the law (religion) is "do." That is the beauty of the gospel—its simplicity. In the insightful words of John Crowder, "Any system of religious belief that puts the emphasis on what you need to do for the Lord, rather than what He has done for you, detracts from the glory of God and spits on the work of the gospel."[3] The law was given until the fullness of time came for Jesus' arrival. It was put in place simply to point us to Jesus. It was introduced to make us realize our need for a savior. Even today, two thousand years later, the noblest of Christian disciplines, such as praying, fasting, worship, and giving, are meant to be our responses of gratitude to His grace and not a means to earn it. Grace cannot be earned; it can only be received as a free gift!

Fourthly, many believers were taught the gospel as if it were God's Plan B. Some believe that the Israelites' continuous disobedience to God—non-observance of the law—led Him to resort to the option of the cross. However, the cross was not introduced because the law failed. The cross has always been Plan A; in fact, it was God's *only* plan. Grace has always been God's chosen method of redemption. Perhaps the law was in effect until people recognized that they could never measure up to God's perfect standard on their own merits. Perhaps grace could not be applied until people gave up on their *futile* human efforts (self-righteous acts) and surrendered to God's gift of grace, realizing their desperate need for a savior.

You see, the cross was God's only plan because the lamb was slain before the foundation of the world (Revelation 13:8). The lamb of God, Christ, was "chosen before the creation of the world, but was revealed in these last times for your sake" (1 Peter 1:18-20, NIV). The purpose of the law and the prophets was to point to the lamb. Jesus was the perfect fulfillment of the law and the prophets. The moment all of Scripture has been pointing to has already arrived! Christ, the mystery of all ages, was unveiled and continues to be unveiled in and through us even today.

> The moment all of Scripture has been pointing to has already arrived! Christ, the mystery of all ages, was unveiled and continues to be unveiled in and through us even today.

Lastly, many of us were taught that the gospel was *just* about salvation. Its message was simply reduced to the atonement and forgiveness of sins—viewed as a means of escape from death and hell, eternal damnation, and one day going to heaven. While salvation is a significant part of the gospel, it is just one aspect. Salvation is the means to an end and not the end in and of itself. We have missed the big picture! Many Christians are merely getting by with the hope of one day making it to heaven, simply surviving rather than thriving, due to a lack of understanding of the gospel. Many know how they are saved (i.e., through Jesus) and from what they are saved (i.e., sin and hell). However, they do not necessarily understand why they are saved (i.e., the purpose of their salvation). (Later in the chapter, we will discuss the symptoms associated with a limited understanding of the gospel.)

So, what is the gospel truly about? Allow me to break

down this ancient mystery using three powerful truths whose revelation and implications should bring about life-altering transformation.

## TRUTH #1 - THE GOSPEL IS ABOUT UNION WITH JESUS

The gospel is about union with Jesus. Our union with Christ—the truth and reality of being made one with Him—is the most profound and glorious truth of the gospel. This is the central theme. If the cross was the means, then our union with Christ eternally is the end. The cross made it possible for us to be cleansed from sin, which was what separated us from God and made us enemies with Him. Therefore, sin had to be dealt with (abolished) on the cross so that Christ may dwell in us and that we may be one with Him in His death and resurrection.

> **If the cross was the means, then our union with Christ eternally is the end.**

"For if we have become **one with Him [permanently united]** in the likeness of His death, we will also certainly be **[one with Him and share fully] in the likeness of His resurrection.** We know that our old self [our human nature without the Holy Spirit] was nailed to the cross with Him, in order that our body of sin might be done away with, so that we would no longer be slaves to sin. For the person who has died [with Christ] has been freed from [the power of] sin. (Romans 6:5-8, AMP, emphasis added)

See also Colossians 2:12-13 and Romans 6:3-4.

87

Even our water baptism is a symbol and declaration of this wonderful truth—a physical demonstration of what already occurred in the spiritual realm, albeit our limited understanding of its implications. We cannot appropriate and live out what we do not know and understand; hence, we need to comprehend our oneness.

Our union with Christ is what qualifies and grants us the mind of Christ (a wealth mindset)—oneness in mind with Christ. Because there is now no separation, this brilliant, excellent mind that is in Christ is now ours for the taking. We can let go of our world programming, our inferior way of thinking (a poverty mindset), for the superior perspective of the Kingdom.

## The Implications of Our Union

Our union with Christ carries significant implications, which we will unpack. Firstly, being united with Christ means we share in His crucifixion and resurrection. This signifies the death of our old, sinful nature alongside Christ and our subsequent rebirth into a newness of life with a new nature. We received a new nature that is reborn and recreated in the image and likeness of Christ. The Bible refers to this transformed being, now in union with Christ, as the new creation. It is Christ in us, the hope of glory (Colossians 1:27), that makes us this new creation. This is the finished work of the cross! This is the privilege and magnificence of the gospel!

"Therefore if anyone is in Christ [that is, grafted in, joined to Him by faith in Him as Savior], he is a new creature [reborn and renewed by the Holy Spirit]; the old things [the previous moral and spiritual condition] have passed away. Behold, new things have come [because spiritual awakening brings a new life]." (2 Corinthians 5:17, AMP)

This new creation, the new you, is not merely a cleaned-up, modified, or improved version of the old man. You are an entirely new being, restored to your original design and true self. Our new nature mirrors Jesus in appearance and essence because we are born from above, belonging to another world. We are no longer *mere* humans. Whether we realize it or not, this truth stands as the reality of our new existence; it is the new order of things for the believer. The new man is not a work in progress; we have already arrived!

> **You are an entirely new being, restored to your original design and true self.**

However, we still need to grow in our understanding of the new man—comprehending what Christ accomplished in and through us. Our minds must be renewed to catch up to this truth. Therefore, "since you have taken off your old self with its practices and have put on the new self, **which is being renewed in knowledge in the image of its Creator.**" (Colossians 3:9-10 NIV, emphasis added).

We simply need to awaken to the truth of our union with Christ—our new nature—to experience its new realities. Our awareness of this union produces a real transformation in us. Christian author and life coach Schlyce Jimenez describes this transformation process: "The outward expression of the new creation, the reality of Christ within, is produced in the lives of believers to the extent that we renew our minds. It's not the truth we hear that sets us free but the truth we come to know experientially."[2]

Secondly, this glorious union with Christ also affords us an eternal connection—a permanent and unbroken fellowship with God through the Holy Spirit (the Spirit of Christ). There is now no separation between God and us, no distance left for us to bridge. The temple curtain (veil) was torn when Jesus finished His work on the cross (Matthew 27:51), granting us *full* access to the Holy of Holies. This signifies our uninterrupted and unconditional access to the presence of God within.

In Christ, we have an open heaven. We live, move, and have our being with God continuously in this glorious entanglement, enjoying an effortless state of "being" in this oneness as opposed to "doing" apart from Him. Any effort on our part to achieve this already-attained union with God (a.k.a., religion) is offensive to the cross, disconnecting us from grace. It attacks the sufficiency of Christ to accomplish this union for us.

> **The new man is not a work in progress; we have already arrived!**

This 24/7 access provided by our union also sets the stage for our ability to communicate with God without interruption, regardless of time or place. This is the context for praying without ceasing, as Scripture highlights (1 Thessalonians 5:16). It goes beyond structured devotion, embracing a moment-by-moment awareness of His indwelling presence. Prayer becomes less about the external activity of articulation and labor and more about an intimate exchange of affection and thoughts. It becomes about revealing the person of Christ within. The only way to walk in step with the Holy Spirit (Galatians 5:16) is to be mature children of God led by the Spirit.

Lastly, our union reveals not only "Christ in us" but also "us in Christ." At salvation, we stepped into Christ. Our new life is now hidden in Christ Jesus (Colossians 3:3), signifying that when the Father looks at us, He sees only Christ. Christ has become our substitute in every way. God no longer sees our former sinful self but Christ's righteousness, which has become our own. He no longer counts our past records (transgressions).

As if that were not enough, being in Christ also means we share in the same love that exists between the Father and the Son, as well as the fellowship they enjoy eternally. As Jesus declares, "'I in them and you in me—so that they may be brought to complete unity. Then the world will know that you sent me and have loved them even as you have loved me'" (John 17:23, NIV). We get the privilege of experiencing this everlasting, life-giving, joyous intimacy with the Godhead, both closely and personally.

Echoing the words of Charles Spurgeon, "There is no joy in this world like union with Christ. The more we can feel it, the happier we are, whatever our circumstances may be."[3]

## TRUTH #2 - THE GOSPEL IS ABOUT THE KINGDOM

The gospel is about the Kingdom of God. Jesus did not come to introduce a religion, not even the religion of Christianity. That's right! He came to introduce the Kingdom of heaven.

The gospels demonstrate that the core of Jesus' message was the Kingdom of God. He Himself openly declared His mission on earth: "'I must preach the good news of the kingdom of God to the other towns as well; for I was sent for this purpose'" (Luke 4:43, ESV).

He signaled the imminent arrival of His Kingdom by urging, "'Repent, for the kingdom of heaven is at hand'" (Matthew 4:17, ESV).

He consistently taught the only way to His Kingdom, asserting, "'Most assuredly, I say to you, unless one is born of water and the Spirit, he cannot enter the kingdom of God'" (John 3:5 NKJV).

He emphasized the importance of the Kingdom, along with its ways and values, instructing, "'But seek first the kingdom of God, and his righteousness; and all these things shall be added unto you'" (Matthew 6:33 KJV).

Dr. Myles Monroe highlights Jesus' emphasis on the Kingdom:

> "Jesus' message, assignment, passion, and purpose were not to establish a religion of rituals and rules but rather to reintroduce a kingdom. Everything Jesus said and did—His prayers, teachings, healings, and miracles—was focused on a kingdom, not a religion. Jesus was preoccupied with the Kingdom; it was His top priority, His heavenly mandate."[4]

Understanding the centrality of the Kingdom ushers us into a different realm, reshaping our way of thinking and functioning. It equips us with a new lens, correcting our vision and fostering in us an abundant mindset as we juxtapose the realities of the Kingdom against those of the world, thereby granting us a better and higher perspective.

## The Centrality of the Kingdom

Despite the centrality of the Kingdom to the gospel message, very little has been taught on the subject in churches and Christian discussions. Many believers view heaven as merely an after-life destination, the final stop following their life journey on earth. Yet, the Kingdom of heaven is not a distant location or a future event. The Kingdom is a "here and now" reality into which we entered the moment we accepted

Christ. The Kingdom represents a spiritual, invisible domain of God: a realm of His presence, available both now and throughout eternity.

The Kingdom of heaven is already within us because the King of the Kingdom, along with His entire dominion, dwells within us through the Holy Spirit. It is crucial to understand that "'the kingdom is not discovered in one place or another, for God's kingdom realm is already expanding within some of you,'" (Luke 17:21, TPT). The reality and manifestations of the Kingdom are only realized when Jesus dwells within us by faith. The immediate accessibility of the King-

> **The Kingdom is a "here and now" reality into which we entered the moment we accepted Christ.**

dom, as opposed to it being a distant promise, enables us to engage with its realities—such as its perspectives, culture, and resources—right here and now.

The Kingdom of heaven is a sovereign country, albeit a spiritual one. Put differently, it is not an earthly or physical kingdom—it comes from another world. As Jesus Himself said: "'My kingdom is not of this world. If it were, my servants would fight to prevent my arrest by the Jews. But now My kingdom is from another place'" (John 18:36, NIV). This Kingdom has a King and a government. The prophet Isaiah foretold the arrival of this King as an infant for the purpose of expanding His spiritual Kingdom on earth.

> "For to us a Child is born, to us a Son is given, and the government will be on His shoulders...Of the increase of His government and peace there will be no end. He will reign on David's throne and over his kingdom, establishing and upholding it with justice and

righteousness from that time on and forever." (Isaiah 9:6-7, NIV)

The purpose of this Kingdom expansion is to include all of humanity into this ever-increasing, ever-thriving, and all-prosperous realm of God. Those who receive Jesus *instantaneously* become eternal citizens of this Kingdom following their spiritual rebirth experience: "We are citizens of Heaven, where the Lord Jesus Christ lives" (Philippians 3:20, NLT). This makes us other-worldly, implying that, akin to any citizenship, we must continually acquaint ourselves with the Kingdom's culture, ideals, principles, and values to flourish within it. It also means we immediately get to enjoy the rights, privileges, and benefits that the Kingdom offers. Our primary allegiance shifts to the Kingdom, superseding any earthly national ties.

> **The purpose of this Kingdom expansion is to include all of humanity into this ever-increasing, ever-thriving, and all-prosperous realm of God.**

There is limited understanding in the church that the Kingdom is distinctly different from religion. In fact, religion is the enemy of the Kingdom. Throughout history, religion has acted as a substitute for the Kingdom—a counterfeit to the Kingdom—hindering people from seeking the authentic solution to their condition. It is no surprise then that Jesus harshly confronted the Pharisees and religious leaders of His day, rebuking them for obstructing the path to His Kingdom:

> "'Woe to you, teachers of the law and Pharisees, you hypocrites! You shut the kingdom of heaven in men's faces. You yourselves do not enter, nor will you let those enter who are trying to.'" (Matthew 23:13, NIV)

The priorities of the Kingdom and religion are always in opposition. It is best described in Dr. Myles Monroe's book *Kingdom Principles*:

"Religion preoccupies man until he finds the Kingdom. Religion is what man does until he finds the Kingdom. Religion prepares man to leave Earth; the Kingdom empowers man to dominate Earth. Religion focuses on Heaven; the Kingdom focuses on Earth. Religion is reaching up to God; the Kingdom is God coming down to man. Religion wants to escape Earth; the Kingdom impacts, influences and changes Earth. Religion seeks to take Earth to Heaven; the Kingdom seeks to bring Heaven to Earth."[5]

Religion defers the Kingdom and our citizenship to a future event, treating it as something to be realized "someday." In contrast, the gospel presents the Kingdom as a current reality, a joy to be embraced now and carried into eternity—this is truly the good news! The Kingdom has already made its entrance on earth through Jesus, leading to its complete unveiling and perfect completion (conclusion) at a future time. Believers can immediately reap its benefits, even amidst this world's imperfections and challenges. We are invited to collaborate with Christ at this very moment to bring heaven on earth in all our situations and expand its reach.

"Jesus came to earth preaching heaven, its riches, its beauty, its infinity, and its availability. He came with the message that there's more to life than what we see— more for those literally disenfranchised and more for those impoverished in their souls. He wasn't a political liberator; He was a spiritual liberator. He came to pronounce freedom from the sin that enslaves and all the eternal consequences it ensures."[6]

## TRUTH #3 - THE GOSPEL IS ABOUT REDEMPTION: THE ORIGINAL MANDATE

The gospel is about redemption, highlighting the singular, redemptive work of Christ accomplished on the cross to save the whole world. Yet, it also refers to the ongoing work of redemption Christ performs in and through us to restore others and creation back to their original design. We were redeemed with the purpose of redeeming others!

> **Redemption is a joint venture with Christ rather than an individual pursuit. It is a collaboration with Him to bring truth, love, grace, and healing to the world.**

In this light, redemption becomes a joint venture with Christ rather than an individual pursuit. It is a collaboration with Him to bring truth, love, grace, and healing to the world. Yet, this is not limited to preaching the gospel in words but putting it into action to restore all things to their redeemed value—their true worth in Christ. This role makes us active participants in the dispensation and unfolding of God's beautiful redemption plan in the world around us.

In practical terms, this translates to Christians becoming agents of positive change inspired by Christ's example. This mission transcends serving within the four walls of the church and supporting missionaries. It encompasses making a tangible impact directly in the world around us across all spheres of influence—be it in business, government, and nonprofit—wherever God has assigned us, despite the decay and deterioration prevalent in the world. This is the very purpose of Christ's sacrifice: "To redeem us from all lawlessness and to purify for himself a people for his own possession who are zealous for good works" (Titus 2:14, NKJV).

For this very reason, all of creation is waiting in eager expectation for the revealing, or uncovering, of the sons of God for such a time as this (Romans 8:19). This entails the mature children of God who embody a wealth mindset, who understand their role as co-partners with Christ in His redemption work—boldly introducing and implementing Kingdom culture and values in the world, despite the limitations and brokenness in the world. They are destined to alter negative culture and perversion, reverse the decay and deterioration, and bring light into dark situations until the day of perfect reconciliation and restoration of all things is achieved in Christ.

### Redemption and the Original Mandate

Remember the original mandate? To trace its origins, we must revisit the Old Testament, back to the genesis of all things. It seems like a distant era, does it not? Our faith journey has brought us to the new covenant, and along this path, some of us may have lost sight of the original mandate. Some may even question its relevance in the New Testament.

In the book of Genesis, God created mankind in His image and gave them the mandate to "be fruitful and multiply, fill the earth and subdue it, and have dominion over the fish of the sea, over the birds of the air, and over every living thing that moves on the earth" (Genesis 1:28, NKJV). In doing so, He declared His purpose and intention for mankind. Yet, after the fall, mankind forfeited its authority and ability to reign and rule over the earth.

Now, fast-forward to the New Testament. Through the redemptive work of Christ, not only are we restored to our original design of His likeness, but also restored to our original mandate (purpose) and are given the opportunity to reign and rule in partnership with Him. We are invited back to the table to participate in the restoration of God's original plan for humanity.

> **We are invited back to the table to participate in the restoration of God's original plan for humanity.**

Redemption, in this context, now closely resembles the mandate to dominate the earthly realm in our spheres of influence and rule over realms of darkness and its evil influences. It transcends personal salvation and seeks to reinstate humanity to its intended role as stewards of creation, individually and collectively.

Now that we have covered what the true gospel entails, let us now examine some of the symptoms associated with a limited understanding of it, which ultimately hinder us from operating in a wealth mindset.

## SYMPTOMS OF LIMITED GOSPEL UNDERSTANDING

These are indicators that a believer with a limited understanding of the gospel may exhibit. Without a proper grasp of the fundamental truths of the gospel, we fall short of fully exhibiting a wealth mindset, missing valuable opportunities to be experienced on this side of eternity.

### 1. Lacking Intimacy.

Believers who lack intimacy with God often perceive Him as distant and unengaged, yet the entire gospel narrative underscores God's redemptive work to win us back to Himself with love and make us His home (His indwelling presence). Deep down, they struggle to truly believe in His goodness towards them, seeing Him more as a taskmaster demanding "perfect" behavior. As a result, they are more focused on following rules and regulations than cultivating a relationship with Him. This leads to a legalistic approach, a substitution for genuine knowledge of God and being known by Him. They relate to Him more as a supreme deity rather than as a Father (Abba), feeling more at ease in the role of God's servants rather than His children. In contrast, "children" recognize their inheritance in Christ and maintain a child-like faith in their Father's provision and abundance, indicative of a wealth mindset. "Servants" lack the intimacy and, thus, the confidence to approach God as their Father, attempting instead to earn His favor through their merit.

## 2. Insecurity.

Believers become insecure in their salvation when they lack understanding of God's grace—the very heart of the gospel. While they may accept God's grace to receive salvation, they often strive to maintain it through their own efforts (actions and behaviors), thereby putting a limit on His grace and undermining the finished work of Christ. They question their salvation whenever they sin or encounter major life challenges. Their inclination is to strive for grace, attempting to earn it rather than accepting it as a free and unlimited gift. In contrast, "secure" believers have the freedom to love, give, do good works, and explore a life of possibilities with God, persuaded by the abundance of His unmerited grace—all attributes of a believer with a wealth mindset—rather than being bound by obligations or appearances.

## 3. Performance-Driven.

Similar to those lacking intimacy with God, believers with a shallow grasp of the gospel often lead lives marked by performance and self-effort instead of grace-empowered obedience. Their relationship with God is characterized by fear, as they have yet to fully comprehend God's perfect love for them—the kind that drives out all fear (1 John 4:18). They struggle to distinguish between holiness and legalism, relying more on self-righteousness rather than Christ's righteousness for their justification. They place a significant emphasis on religious practices, adherence to moral codes, or personal achievements as a basis for evaluating their standing with God. In contrast, believers grounded in the gospel understand their oneness with Christ is the source of their holiness and righteousness, freeing them from the need to strive. This connection to the abundant Source allows them to rest from performance, allowing them to embody a mindset of wealth.

### 4. Sin-Focused.

When believers have an incomplete understanding of the gospel, they become sin-conscious (Romans 3:20) rather than righteousness-conscious (Romans 3:21-22). They exert tremendous effort trying to eradicate sin from their lives and purify themselves rather than accepting the righteousness that comes from God by faith. They have yet to realize that they already possess the righteousness of God in Christ Jesus, which empowers them to live in righteousness. Their sin consciousness often leads them to a continuous struggle with sin as they rely on their own strength to overcome it. In contrast, believers who are rooted in the gospel know they are already dead to sin and alive to righteousness in Christ (Romans 6:11), reflecting the beliefs and thought patterns associated with a wealth mindset.

### 5. Heaven-Bound.

When believers are not taught the gospel correctly, they focus too much on going to heaven, making them less effective for earth. Instead of manifesting heaven on earth to impact and influence it, they seek to escape earth. This contrasts with the idea of setting our minds on things above, and not on earthly things (Colossians 3:2), which encourages a focus on eternal, spiritual perspectives over temporal, earthly concerns. It is important to note that it is healthy to yearn for a better (even perfect) world and anticipate the return of Jesus Christ. Jesus commissions us to engage with the world, not withdraw from it—to extend the Kingdom's influence outward. Conversely, believers well-versed in the gospel recognize their earthly mission to bring about positive change. They are aware of their mandate to dominate and impact the earth through the Kingdom that they carry within.

As we conclude this chapter, remember: the gospel extends beyond salvation—beyond being rescued from sin and hell. Primarily, we have established that the gospel is about our union with Christ, making us new creations with a new nature like God's, forever changing our position in Christ. The gospel is about the coming of God's Kingdom on earth, residing within us and expanding into the world through us. Additionally, the gospel is about redemption—God's agenda to restore mankind and all of creation, an agenda that has now become ours as we co-partner with Christ in this endeavor, and a renewal of our original mandate to reign and dominate the earth with God. A profound comprehension of the gospel enables us to adopt a wealth mindset.

In the next chapter, we will discuss the nature of God, laying another building block for cultivating an abundance mindset.

## CHAPTER 5

# Knowing God

IN ONE OF my encounters with God, I was in a vision where I found myself transported to the vast expanse of the cosmos that left me awestruck. In the vision, I stood face-to-face with a man who I knew was Jesus. As our eyes met, it was as if we were able to communicate without words, transcending language, our connection flowing seamlessly through the silent exchange of thoughts and emotions. Suddenly, the ground beneath me completely gave way, vanishing into thin air. For a moment, I was disoriented, trying to find my footing. After a short while, I realized I was able to float, suspended in the air without dropping down; gravity had no effect on me.

Although we were surrounded by the darkness of night, the heavens above shimmered with the brilliance of countless stars and other celestial things. Together, we started on an exploration through the cosmos where Jesus unveiled the breathtaking wonders of His creation. Every sight, every revelation, left me utterly dumbfounded, my senses overwhelmed by the sheer magnificence of it all.

Right in the middle of our journey, Jesus paused, turned to me, and said, "You know, you can stand?" At His words, I dared to rest my foot on the invisible void beneath me—to my astonishment, I found I was able to stand—and stand firm—as if there was a sturdy glass floor under my feet.

In the months and years that followed that extraordinary vision, my life unfolded much like the scenes in the vision, mirroring the journey I had experienced with Jesus. Everything I had once deemed solid and secure—everything I had assumed was permanent—began to fall apart before my eyes. In this place of uncertainty, I struggled to find my bearings, feeling confused as the familiar landmarks of my life faded into obscurity. In those dark moments, when I could hardly recognize the life I once knew, Jesus was there with me as a constant presence amid the chaos.

Together, Jesus and I embarked on a remarkable journey, exploring the mysteries of His Kingdom with a sense of awe and wonder, just as in the vision. In the hallowed moments we shared, Jesus would share His heart with me, revealing deep truths and secrets that illuminated the path ahead. Despite the pain and turmoil that surrounded me, His presence brought a perfect peace and unspeakable joy beyond measure, transforming even the darkest moments into some of the most cherished, memorable, and defining times of my life.

One day, I found myself standing firm and grounded, even in the midst of chaos and tremendous loss, anchored *not* in the certainty and security of life but in the unchanging and unshakeable nature of God. I remembered the words of Jesus that I could stand even without an underlying structure holding me. In that moment of revelation, I realized that Jesus Christ alone (and His word) was my foundation! Even during life's disruptions, He is the solid rock I stand upon!

This is the God we worship!

## HIS HIGHEST PRIORITY

The goal of our journey as Christians lies in the pursuit of knowing God intimately—becoming deeply acquainted with His nature, ways, and will: "Now this is eternal life, that they know you the only true God, and Jesus Christ whom you have sent" (John 17:3, NIV). The cross, therefore, stands as the ultimate testament to the significance of knowing God, for through it, we gain access to the profound depths of His character and purpose.

> "And we know that the Son of God has come, and has given us understanding so that we may know Him who is true; and we are in Him who is true, in His Son Jesus Christ. This is the true God and eternal life." (1 John 5:20, NKJV)

Knowing God is thus the true meaning of life. It entails cultivating a thriving inner (spiritual) life that is characterized by a genuine, active, and vigorous relationship that exudes a deep sense of vitality (aliveness) and fulfillment, all rooted in an intimate connection with God. This profound reality is vividly depicted by the metaphor of rivers of living water flowing within us in our innermost parts, symbolizing the indwelling presence of the Holy Spirit, who promotes this intimate communion with the triune God (John 7:38).

**Knowing God is thus the true meaning of life.**

Everything else we engage in, whether it be worship, service, or any other Christian practice, stems from this intimate acquaintance with God or exists to foster one. We cannot genuinely and fully worship someone we do not know, nor can we authentically serve a God who is a stranger to us.

Without this knowledge, we merely go through religious motions, adhering to norms and regulations, devoid of genuine connection. It is in knowing God intimately that our faith transcends religious performance, leading us into a meaningful relationship with our Creator.

Yet, what exactly does this knowledge imply? It surely transcends *mere* intellectual or theological knowledge about God. It goes beyond knowing the word of God—memorizing Scripture or reciting Bible verses. There is a crucial distinction between knowing *about* God and genuinely knowing God Himself—one involves acquiring information, while the other requires a close, personal relationship. In this case, I am referring to an *experiential knowledge* of God because knowledge divorced from personal experience holds little value.

> We cannot genuinely and fully worship someone we do not know, nor can we authentically serve a God who is a stranger to us.

In this context, the term "knowledge" originates from the Greek word *ginóskō* and is a prolonged form of "to know," resulting from a long or extended practice. It signifies knowledge acquired through direct experience and close proximity to the subject—an understanding grounded in personal encounters as opposed to simple theoretical learning or second-hand information.

Furthermore, while this form of knowledge may originate in the mind, starting with information and intellect, it goes much deeper—it involves knowing in the heart. The Bible frequently refers to it as understanding or revelation: the ability to see or perceive with our spiritual eyes what is unseen. This revelation knowledge ignites faith within us, which leads to wisdom and inspires action. It is the pathway to trusting and loving God and being persuaded of His goodness. It makes us rejoice in God, giving Him the highest glory: "God is most glorified in you when you are most satisfied in Him," as John Piper often articulates.[1] Such knowledge instills within us a reverence (the fear of the Lord) arising from awe and wonder.

This experiential and revelation knowledge of God becomes the lens through which we view all aspects of life. It shapes our perception of self, given that our identity originates from Him. This knowledge of God influences our interpretation of life's events, defining our purpose and destiny. It corrects the lens through which we understand and interpret Scriptures and deepens our trust in Him and His promises, thereby impacting our capacity to receive from Him. Ultimately, it shapes our mindset, governing our thoughts and actions and determining whether we operate with a wealth mindset. Therefore, as believers, it is crucial that we continually grow in the knowledge of God to renew our minds.

## GOD'S NATURE REVEALED

In the Old Testament, God was known by various names, each reflecting a different aspect of His character and nature: the Lord our Shepherd, Banner (or victory), Healer, Righteousness, Provider, and Peace.

In the New Testament, we witness a profound elevation and amplification of these same divine attributes, albeit expressed in a renewed manner. In this section, we will focus on three key aspects of His nature that help to promote a wealth mindset.

### 1. God Our Savior and Redeemer

One of the predominant attributes of God emphasized in the New Testament is His role as the Savior—the Messiah or the Christ. Knowing God as Savior involves recognizing Him as the one who rescues, delivers, and saves humanity from the power and consequences of sin. Although in the Old Testament God intervened to save the Israelites from their enemies on occasion, in the New Testament, rescuing the entire human race once and for all was the entire mission of His incarnation.

Jesus' work on the cross was not to save us from the Father's wrath but to save us for Himself. It was not to appease an angry God (Father) who desired to punish us for our disobedience but to win our affection through His sacrificial love. Sin is its own punishment! God's heart is always inclined towards us, not against us. His focus is on the destructive nature of sin in us—the penalty and the damage it inflicts by separating us from Him. God despises sin, not the sinner.

**Sin is its own punishment!**

His mission was not only to save and rescue us from sin by destroying the entire body of sin but to redeem us to our former glory. Knowing God as Redeemer involves understanding His work of delivering and restoring us to our original design, worth, and innocence. It is recognizing His transformative power in bringing renewal and wholeness to us, reversing the works of evil in humanity and overall creation. John Crowder explains it like this:

"In Jesus Christ, we see that God is not the bringer of evil, but the redeemer from evil. He allows our liberty, foreseeing our error, with the rescue, redemption and restoration of humanity summed up in Christ from before our very creation."[2]

God's rescue and redemption work publicly demonstrated and revealed the depths of His love and grace. For God's love was the driving force behind His redemptive plan, as expressed in His assumption of human form and His role as our substitution, both as us and for us (John 3:16). His justice was perfectly satisfied through the atoning work of Christ, fulfilling divine righteousness (Romans 3:26).

### God of Grace and Truth

A natural extension of God's nature as savior and redeemer is His nature as the God of grace and truth. Scripture emphasizes that Jesus came full of grace and truth: "For the law was given through Moses, but grace and truth came through Jesus Christ" (John 1:17, NKJV). Jesus embodies grace and truth perfectly, with neither ever compromised in the slightest.

With grace, God offered Himself in our place by becoming our substitute on the cross and our righteousness, uniting Himself with us to make us a new creation in Him. He also extends forgiveness of sins to all who believe. With truth, He made the world aware of its sinful and hopeless condition, pointing it to the Truth Himself: Jesus. In truth, He redirects and reorients His children back to Himself and their original design in Him.

Much of the church today tends to lean either toward grace (grace-focused) or truth (truth-focused), often missing the mark in reflecting God's true nature. When we lack grace, we risk becoming legalistic and judgmental, entangled in self-righteousness. We distort God's loving and accepting nature, misrepresenting Him in the world. While there is no concept of "ultra" grace (as grace itself is inherently extravagant), when not partnered with truth, it loses its essence. Conversely, without truth, we risk being shapeless and in disarray, lacking integrity and standards, and misrepresenting God's righteousness and holiness.

While the cross stands as the greatest display of grace and truth, every interaction Jesus had with people showcased this aspect of His character. A striking illustration of this is found in John 8, where the Pharisees brought a woman caught in adultery before Jesus in an attempt to test and trap Him. Jesus responds to them:

> "'He who is without sin among you, let him throw a stone at her first.' And again He stooped down and wrote on the ground. Then those who heard it, being convicted by their conscience, went out one by one, beginning with the oldest even to the last. And Jesus was left alone, and the woman standing in the midst. When Jesus had raised Himself up and saw no one but the woman, He said to her, **'Woman, where are those accusers of yours? Has no one condemned you?'** She said, 'No one, Lord.' And Jesus said to her, **'Neither do I condemn you; go and sin no more.'**" (John 8: 7-11, NKJV, emphasis added)

Jesus showed perfect grace toward the woman whom the religious and legalistic leaders wanted to condemn to death. However, He did not overlook her sinful condition; He elevated her status by speaking the truth—to go and sin no more. He extends the same grace and truth to us as believers. Growing to the full measure and stature of Jesus Christ involves embracing the fullness of His grace and truth, not just one or the other, but both through our union with Him.

*God as Savior and Redeemer and a Wealth Mindset*
Believers with a wealth mindset are anchored in God's saving and redeeming work on the cross. They recognize that, through Christ's redemptive work, they have already been restored to

their original design—finding their worth and innocence in Him. They actively participate in Christ's redemptive work, applying it to themselves and in the world while bringing transformation and renewal. Being convinced that God is always for them and not against them, they continuously grow in the richness of God's grace and truth, accurately representing His nature.

## 2. God our Father

When Jesus ushered in the new covenant of grace, He introduced a revolutionary concept of God as Father. While in the Old Testament, God was understood as the Father of a nation (Israel), Jesus revealed Him as the perfect and personal Father in the New Testament. Through Christ, we now have the privilege of experiencing an intimate Father-child relationship that extends through eternity.

Jesus, as God incarnate, became the perfect mirror through which we know the invisible God, the Father, for to see Jesus is to see the Father (Hebrews 1:3). He is the exact representation and imprint of the character and nature of God the Father. In Jesus, we see the goodness of the Father revealed, not only through His character during His earthly ministry but also in the redemptive plan orchestrated by the Father through the incarnation, wherein Jesus came in human likeness to rescue the world. This act shows the Father's heart toward humanity.

The truth is that God is a good Father. He is the origin of everything good (Mark 10:18); not only does He perform good deeds, speak good words, and bestow good gifts, but goodness is inherent to His nature (see Psalm 119:68 and James 1:17). He is not some distant, angry, disapproving, or demanding Father, nor is He a harsh taskmaster wielding a whip. His disposition is not one of negativity or ill-will. Do not allow your past experiences with imperfect earthly fathers to distort your perception of your perfect heavenly Father and His unfathomable goodness.

God's goodness must undergird our entire belief system. It should be the basis for all theology because Jesus Christ, the perfect display of God's goodness, is perfect theology. It ought to be the filter through which we understand and interpret all of Scripture. Even the challenging and seemingly harsh passages and narratives from the Old Testament, when viewed through the lens of God's goodness, begin to transform and take on a beautiful shape rather than being viewed through our limited human judgment. Even God's wrath emerges as an expression of His goodness and love. Because God's character remains constant, the same God revealed in Jesus Christ in the New Testament is the same God of the Old Testament. He is the same yesterday, today, and forever.

> God's goodness must undergird our entire belief system.

Even our life circumstances, particularly the negative ones, must be framed and interpreted through the lens of God's goodness. You may have encountered difficult or traumatic situations in the past or are currently suffering a loss that makes you question God's goodness. While acknowledging that this perspective is not always easy to maintain, it is essential to define our circumstances in the context of His overarching goodness, even in moments of confusion. As Bill Johnson puts it, "Seeing His goodness assures us that no matter what's happening, it is going to turn out for His glory and our strength."[3]

Often, it is only in retrospect that we grasp the broader picture, realizing that our trials often conceal blessings in disguise. Remember, "In all things God works together for the good of those who love him" (Romans 8:28, NIV). Even in moments of uncertainty or lack of understanding, let His goodness be your anchor.

His goodness serves not just as the basis of all theology, but as the bedrock and source of all His other attributes—His love, kindness, grace, mercy, generosity, patience, faithfulness, righteousness, and more. His goodness is not just an aspect of His character; rather, it encapsulates the entirety and summation of all His attributes.

**His goodness serves not just as the basis of all theology, but as the bedrock and source of all His other attributes.**

And God said, "I will **make all My goodness pass before you,** and I will proclaim the Name of the LORD before you; **for I will be gracious to whom I will be gracious, and will show compassion (lovingkindness) on whom I will show compassion.**" (Exodus 33:19, AMP, emphasis added)

"[Then] the Lord passed before him and proclaimed, "The Lord, the Lord, a God **merciful and gracious, slow to anger, and abounding in steadfast love and faithfulness.**" (Exodus 34:6, ESV, emphasis added)

"He loves righteousness and justice; the earth is full of the goodness of the Lord." (Psalm 33:5, NKJV)

"The Lord is good to all, and His tender mercies are over all His works." (Psalm 145:9, NKJV)

Even His holiness is not in conflict with His goodness; they work in perfect tandem. The cross stands as the perfect expression of God's goodness and holiness—where His righteous requirements were fully met in Jesus while demonstrating His goodness in the redemption of humanity. In the words of Bill Johnson, "God is good all the way through. He is as good as he is holy."[4]

God's goodness transcends mere intellectual knowledge. While many Christians acknowledge that God is good in a general sense, few truly internalize, comprehend, and sense His goodness to their core. Even fewer genuinely believe that His goodness extends to them personally. How about you? Do you struggle with believing and receiving His goodness? His goodness is something to be perceived and encountered. The Psalmist beautifully expresses: "O taste and see that the LORD is good: Blessed is the man who trusts in Him!" (Psalm 34:8, NKJV)

It is intriguing that David extends this invitation to perceive and experience God's goodness precisely when he was in hiding, pursued by King Saul, who sought to take his life. David's unwavering belief in God's goodness formed the foundation of his trust in Him, even amidst adversity. Similarly, our confidence in His goodness influences our interaction and relationship with God. It impacts our level of trust and our ability to rest in Him without feeling anxious, fearful, or depressed. When we are convinced of His goodness, hope becomes our default stance, and this hope never fails us. Ultimately, His goodness shapes our reality and directs our destiny.

Fortunately, His goodness is not dependent on us; it is not tied to our performance or efforts. It's an inherent aspect of His nature; it defines who He is! However, our belief in His goodness determines how much of His goodness we will experience in this life. The more we trust in His goodness, the more we witness its manifestation in our lives. John Crowder writes:

"You will get out of God what you believe about Him. Believe He is harsh and that is what will manifest in your life. Believe He is good and you will experience His goodness. Let it be according to your faith."[5]

"Oh, how great is Your goodness, which You have laid up for those who fear You, which You have prepared for those who trust in You in the presence of the sons of men! You shall hide them in the secret place of Your presence from the plots of man; You shall keep them secretly in a pavilion from the strife of tongues." (Psalm 31:19-20 NKJV)

## The Cost of Unbelief in God's Goodness

Without being grounded in the understanding of God's goodness, we will fall prey to the enemy's schemes and his age-long strategy of deception—sowing seeds of doubt regarding God's goodness. When we succumb to the enemy's lies and question God's goodness, our ability to trust God weakens, hindering our capacity to stand firm in faith and perseverance. This erodes our confidence in His promises, ultimately derailing us from the good path He has set before us.

Remember the enemy's oldest trick in the Garden of Eden? In the Genesis 3 account, Satan planted a seed of doubt in Eve, causing her to question God's goodness and integrity. He insinuated that God was not for but against them. Once Eve became convinced that God's intentions were not good, her trust in Him faltered, leading her to partake of the forbidden fruit—the very thing God forbade for their protection.

"Now the serpent was more crafty (subtle, skilled in deceit) than any living creature of the field which the

Lord God had made. And the serpent (Satan) said to the woman, 'Can it really be that God has said, "You shall not eat from any tree of the garden"?' And the woman said to the serpent, 'We may eat fruit from the trees of the garden, except the fruit from the tree which is in the middle of the garden. God said, "You shall not eat from it nor touch it, otherwise you will die."' But the serpent said to the woman, 'You certainly will not die! For God knows that on the day you eat from it your eyes will be opened [that is, you will have greater awareness], and you will be like God, knowing [the difference between] good and evil.' And when the woman saw that the tree was good for food, and that it was delightful to look at, and a tree to be desired in order to make one wise and insightful, she took some of its fruit and ate it; and she also gave some to her husband with her, and he ate. Then the eyes of the two of them were opened [that is, their awareness increased], and they knew that they were naked; and they fastened fig leaves together and made themselves coverings." (Genesis 3: 1-7, AMP, emphasis added)

Similarly, we see the same pattern repeated by the Israelites in the wilderness—their doubt and unbelief in God's goodness leading to complaining and grumbling, and eventually disobedience, prolonging their stay in the desert to forty years instead of forty days. Despite God's miraculous provisions and interventions, they persisted in unbelief, hindering them from entering the promised land—God's rest (Hebrews 3:19). This pattern of unbelief in God's goodness remains a common and primary scheme of the enemy today, diverting us from our faith and from entering into God's rest.

Therefore, it is essential that we firmly settle in our minds and hearts once and for all the unwavering goodness of God—not only towards us collectively as the church but also individually. A mind continually renewed by the reality of God's goodness remains steadfast even in the face of negative circumstances and trials that seek to challenge it. For the mind that consistently dwells on His goodness will experience its abundant fruits: "God will keep in perfect and constant peace the one whose mind is steadfast [that is, committed and focused on You—in both [inclination and character], Because he trusts and takes refuge in You [with hope and confident expectation]" (Isaiah 26:3, AMP).

A firm conviction in God's goodness becomes a vital weapon in our arsenal to thwart and stand against the devil's schemes. Like a shield in the armor of God, our faith in His goodness safeguards our entire being, ensuring our overall well-being. I am more convinced than ever that the essence of our spiritual warfare—the good fight of faith—lies in steadfastly fixing our gaze on God's goodness, regardless of the circumstances.

> A mind continually renewed by the reality of God's goodness remains steadfast even in the face of negative circumstances and trials that seek to challenge it.

The challenge lies in keeping this truth at the forefront of our minds as we navigate life with God, both in the good and bad times. Even when we stumble and lose sight of His goodness amid life's storms, our task is to fight our way back and refocus our gaze back on His goodness, echoing the attitude expressed by King David in his song: "I would have lost heart, unless I had believed that I would see the goodness of the Lord in the land of the living" (Psalm 27:13 NKJV).

*The Father's Heart*

The goodness of the Father captures the essence of His heart, reflecting His good thoughts and intentions towards us. It is His "genetic" makeup. Throughout His teachings and parables, Jesus revealed the nature of His Father. One remarkable example that stands out in revealing the Father's heart marked by His goodness is the Parable of the Prodigal Son (Luke15:11-32).

As a reminder, we have already established that God's goodness encompasses the sum of all His attributes.

In the story, the father symbolizes God the Father, with his character and attitude mirroring the heart of the Father. In the beginning, we observe the youngest son's audacious request for his inheritance, to which the father responds by dividing his estate between his sons and granting the request despite its outrageous nature (as inheritances were typically not distributed until the father's passing in Jewish culture). This portrayal reflects the father's goodness, demonstrated through his love, as he allows his son to exercise his choice and respects his decision without imposing control or manipulation. Similarly, God the Father expresses His love by granting us the freedom to choose Him and His ways or our own, honoring our free will.

Later on, we witness the son squandering his money in reckless living, ultimately finding himself destitute. Upon recognizing his errors, he resolves to return home with hopes of securing a position among his father's servants, convinced that his father would be good enough to at least provide for his servants and treat them kindly. Little did he know he was about to discover firsthand just how exceedingly good his father truly was!

"But while he [the son] was still a long way off, his father saw him and was filled with compassion for him; he ran to his son, threw his arms around him and kissed him." (Luke 15:20, NIV)

Here, we see the father's goodness expressed in his mercy and grace towards his son, despite all the contempt, shame, and pain the son had inflicted upon him—a kindness the son did not deserve. Instead of condemnation or vindication, the father was moved with compassion. He had already forgiven his son before the son even had the chance to confess and seek forgiveness. Still, we witness the father's goodness manifested in his complete disregard (reckless abandon) for his dignity as he ran towards his son, embracing him in his filth and destitution, throwing himself at his son and showering him with affection, overjoyed at his return.

Similarly, our Father in heaven, regardless of our performance or behavior, always yearns for our return to Him—our true Home. He longs for our company. We are constantly on His mind; His thoughts towards us are precious and too numerous to count (Psalm 139:17). He relentlessly pursues us with extravagant and "reckless" love, even in the face of our resistance and rejection. Amidst our struggles and hardships—whether self-inflicted or otherwise—He desires to walk alongside us, embracing us with His love and kindness (if we let Him). He does not orchestrate tragedies or bring disaster upon us, but at times, He allows us to endure them while working to redeem the situation and reverse its effects. He promises to bring good out of every tragedy and to administer justice as we remain in Him. He wastes no pain!

Even when the son was tempted to renounce or abandon his identity as a son, haunted by his past mistakes and failures, and considered taking on the role and identity of another, a slave or servant, the father continued to see him as his beloved son and treated him accordingly. He adorned him with a robe, a symbol of dignity and honor, placed a ring on his finger to affirm his status, and provided him with shoes, reinstating him to his rightful position. The father rejoiced at his son's return and celebrated with a grand feast.

> "The son said to him, '**Father, I have sinned against heaven and against you. I am no longer worthy to be called your son.**' But the father said to his servants, 'Quick! Bring the best robe and put it on him. Put a ring on his finger and sandals on his feet. Bring the fattened calf and kill it. Let's have a feast and celebrate. For this son of mine was dead and is alive again; he was lost and is found.' So they began to celebrate. (Luke 15: 21-24, NIV, emphasis added)

In the same way, our Father, in His boundless grace and unconditional love, joyfully restores us to our rightful position, regardless of our past mistakes. He celebrates us and our continuous decision to believe and embrace Him anew.

Lastly, we observe the father's goodness in his patience toward and acceptance of the oldest son, who reacted with self-righteousness and indignation. Despite always being "around" the father, the eldest son failed to grasp his father's goodness. He believed he was entitled to his father's blessings and inheritance due to his "perfect" performance. He had yet to realize that his father's wealth was also his to enjoy and steward. Though a son, he too harbored a slave mentality.

> "The older brother became angry and refused to go in. So his father went out and pleaded with him. But he answered his father, 'Look! All these years I've been

slaving for you and never disobeyed your orders. Yet you never gave me even a young goat so I could celebrate with my friends. But when this son of yours who has squandered your property with prostitutes comes home, you kill the fattened calf for him!' 'My son,' the father said, 'you are always with me, and everything I have is yours. But we had to celebrate and be glad, because this brother of yours was dead and is alive again; he was lost and is found.'" (Luke 15:28-31, NIV)

## God as Father and a Wealth Mindset

Believers with a wealth mindset have experienced God as a Father and are deeply persuaded of His goodness. They understand the reality of having a good Father who loves and desires to care for them. Consequently, they rely on Him rather than solely on their ability to provide for themselves and fulfill their needs. They have shed their "orphan spirit," no longer living with a fatherless mentality. Fear and anxiety do not dominate their lives as they once did because they know that such attitudes are an insult to the very nature of God: His goodness.

They recognize that every good thing comes from the Father and thus attribute all their blessings to Him, refusing to take credit, giving glory to God instead. Viewing life through the lens of His goodness, they opt to trust Him even amidst life's trials. Their minds remain fixed on His goodness, even when faced with perplexing circumstances. They exemplify those whom the Bible calls blessed.

"Blessed is the one who trusts in the Lord, whose confidence is in him. They will be like a tree planted by the water that sends out its roots by the stream. It does not fear when heat comes; its leaves are always green. It has no worries in a year of drought and never fails to bear fruit." (Jeremiah 17:7-8, NIV)

### 3. God our Source

From the dawn of creation, we see God as the Source of all things. Every good thing finds its origin in Him: "Yet for us there is [only] one God, the Father, who is the Source of all things" (1 Corinthians 8:6, AMPC). Knowing God as the Source means recognizing Him as the inexhaustible, all-sufficient, abundant provider—the blessed God. It involves believing and acknowledging by faith that He is our sole Source for all our needs.

> **God's supply is not automatic! . . . We fail to receive *fully* from the Source because we rely on "alternative" sources—other people and things that we have elevated to the status of primary providers instead of God Himself.**

God is the everlasting Source that never runs dry. When we are connected to this unlimited Source continually, we are full to overflow, never running out. Consider the electrical outlet in your home. There is an enormous supply of electric power behind it. Yet, unless your electronic devices are plugged into the outlet—the source—they will not function, hindering you from accessing and utilizing the available power. Similarly, God's supply is not automatic! Unless we remain continuously connected, fully aware that God is our sole and true Source, we cannot access all that He has made available to us. Faith is the conduit through which we plug into and access this Source.

Typically, we fail to receive *fully* from the Source because we rely on "alternative" sources—other people and things that we have elevated to the status of primary providers instead of

God Himself. Consider if your job (salary) or business is your source of income and security; your family the source of love, acceptance, and satisfaction; or your work the source of fulfillment and significance. Do not be deceived! In the words of Tony Evans, "God is the source. Everything else is a resource."[6]

Your job only serves as the channel through which God provides financially. Your family and friends offer glimpses of God's nature (face) and blessings in your life, allowing you to experience love and connection, but they cannot be depended on as the primary source. God is the ultimate Source! Unfortunately, sometimes we may not fully recognize or experience the true Source until these alternative sources dry up.

> **God is the true Source of our spiritual, emotional (soul) as well as physical (material) needs.**

According to Philippians 4:19 (AMPC), "God will liberally supply (fill to the full) your every need according to His riches in glory in Christ Jesus." While this Scripture is commonly associated with physical or financial needs, human needs encompass more than just material. Our deepest needs often lie in the spiritual and emotional realms. God is the true Source of our spiritual, emotional (soul) as well as physical (material) needs.

## Our Spiritual Needs
Primarily, God is the source of our spiritual needs. These needs are not met *just once* at salvation but as an ongoing process of replenishment. As believers, our deepest need and desire is God Himself. He satisfies our innermost being in a way nothing else can. God is the source of eternal life—the life of God that flows in and through us in Christ, also known as "Zoë" in the Greek. This Zoë life within us signifies a spiritual life

that is abundant, everlasting, and full of vitality. It is manifested through the Holy Spirit—the Spirit of Christ—whom Jesus promised to give to those who believe in Him.

> "'But whoever drinks the water that I give him will never be thirsty again. But the water that I give him will become in him a spring of water [**satisfying his thirst for God**] welling up [continually flowing, bubbling within him] to eternal life.'" (John 4:14, AMP, emphasis added)

> "Jesus stood and said in a loud voice, 'Let anyone who is thirsty come to me and drink. Whoever believes in me, as Scripture has said, **rivers of living water will flow from within them.**' By this he meant the Spirit, whom those who believed in him were later to receive." (John 7:37–39, NIV, emphasis added)

**In that sacred space of intimate presence, we are filled and refilled with His perfect peace and indescribable joy, finding our true rest in Him.**

The Holy Spirit is the abundant life within us—the river that runs deep, quenching our thirst for God. However, merely having the Holy Spirit indwelling us does not automatically mean we are "drinking" from Him, fully tapping into His supply. Like the electric outlet analogy where electronics must be connected to the power source to function, His presence does not guarantee our engagement or utilization.

The key to drawing from the Source is to abide in His presence and receive by faith—being awakened to and consciously aware of His indwelling presence. Jesus teaches us, saying, "I am the vine, you are the branches. He who abides in Me, and I in him, bears much fruit; for without Me you can do nothing" (John 15:5 NKJV). Just as a branch needs to remain connected to the vine to receive its nourishment (sap), we, too, must continue in His presence, drinking deeply and being filled with the Spirit to produce His fruits. It involves remaining focused and keenly aware of His intimate presence and engaging with Him.

In that sacred space of intimate presence, we are filled and refilled with His perfect peace and indescribable joy, finding our true rest in Him. It is where we receive affirmation of our identity in Christ and awaken to our oneness with our source of righteousness and holiness, bearing the fruit of righteousness and holiness in our lives. Here, we find deep satisfaction in life despite our external circumstances, bearing the fruit of contentment. We are bestowed with wisdom from above. In this place, we thrive internally as we experience this deeper life with God, even amidst pain and loss.

> **His intimate presence stands as our ultimate reward and greatest blessing in life!**

His intimate presence, which never departs or forsakes us, surpasses any temporal blessings such as familial bonds, financial prosperity, or physical well-being. It stands as our ultimate reward and greatest blessing in life!

## Our Emotional Needs
God is also the ultimate source of our emotional needs, abundantly meeting the yearnings of our souls in His presence:

> "Oh, that men would give thanks to the Lord for His goodness, and for His wonderful works to the children

of men! For He [God] satisfies the longing soul, and fills the hungry soul with goodness." (Psalm 107:9, ESV)

Whether they are needs for purpose, meaning and significance (uniqueness), love and connection (vulnerability), worth, acceptance, security, or strength, they can be fulfilled by God if we allow Him. People can provide emotional support from time to time; however, relying solely on them to satisfy these needs will inevitably leave us feeling unsatisfied and overly dependent. As adults, being overly needy towards others is unbecoming and undesirable, but neediness towards God (dependence) is not only acceptable but also necessary. We are designed to derive our nourishment from Him, much like branches are designed to draw sap from the vine.

Our ability to emotionally pour into others hinges on our continuous filling in His presence. We can only encourage and care for others when we are replenished ourselves. When our soul is refreshed, we refresh others in turn. Otherwise, we run the risk of living as "zombies"—depleted, lifeless, and apathetic (lacking in feelings, interest, or concern for the things that matter).

Our needs are meant to point us to God. In fact, they are necessary vehicles leading us to Him, cultivating an intimate relationship that compels us to continually seek His refills. They usher us into His presence, where we seek and find true fulfillment in Christ. In encountering Him, we receive His boundless love, which becomes the foundation for loving ourselves and others. We experience a sense of worth and acceptance, making us bold and confident. We find strength and hope, and our hearts are filled with joy and peace. Conversely, in His presence, fear dissolves, depression melts away, anxiousness subsides, insecurity vanishes, and loneliness disappears.

*Our Physical Needs*

Lastly, God is the source of our physical and material needs. He is concerned about our physical well-being as much as He does for our spiritual and emotional needs. During His earthly ministry, Jesus exemplified this care by feeding multitudes and healing the sick.

Through His actions and teaching, Jesus consistently revealed the Father's goodness, showcasing His desire and ability to provide for His beloved children. In one of His teachings, Jesus vividly illustrates our immense worth to the Father as His cherished offspring compared to all other creations:

"'Therefore I tell you, do not be anxious about your life, what you will eat or what you will drink, nor about your body, what you will put on. Is not life more than food, and the body more than clothing? Look at the birds of the air: they neither sow nor reap nor gather into barns, and yet your heavenly Father feeds them. Are you not of more value than they?... Consider the lilies of the field, how they grow: they neither toil nor spin, yet I tell you, even Solomon in all his glory was not arrayed like one of these. But if God so clothes the grass of the field, which today is alive and tomorrow is thrown into the oven, will he not much more clothe you, O you of little faith? Therefore do not be anxious, saying, "What shall we eat?" or "What shall we drink?" or "What shall we wear?" For the Gentiles seek after all these things, and your heavenly Father knows that you need them all.'" (Matthew 6:25-26, 28-32, ESV)

Similar to our spiritual and emotional needs, God's provision for our physical well-being is received and accessed through faith. It is not automatic! While His grace makes it available for all, our child-like trust and dependence, demonstrated by our lack of fear, worry, and anxiousness, draws the supply. Faith is what activates and unleashes the provision, not the mere existence of our needs.

*God as the Source and a Wealth Mindset*

Believers with a wealth mindset are firmly rooted in the belief that God is their primary Source for all their spiritual, emotional, and physical needs. They not only recognize God as their Source but also understand His abundance, limitlessness, and all-sufficiency (Philippians 4:19). They acknowledge that every good thing they possess comes from Him (Psalm 16:2).

> **Faith is what activates and unleashes the provision, not the mere existence of our needs.**

They have learned to depend on and draw from the Source through faith by abiding in His presence. They find their nourishment and satisfaction in life through the Holy Spirit to meet their deepest needs. They have cultivated a child-like trust in God to receive His provision for all their needs. Above all, they realize that all good things are *from*, *through*, and *for* Him (Romans 11:36).

In conclusion, the pursuit of intimately knowing God stands not only as the highest priority of our lives but also as a foundational step in cultivating a wealth mindset. By renewing our minds with a deep understanding of God's nature—primarily His redemptive quality, His goodness as a Father, and His nature as our abundant Source—our beliefs and perspectives on God will be transformed, resulting in an abundance mindset.

In the upcoming chapter, we will examine how understanding our identity serves as another building block in cultivating a wealth mindset. We will explore how our experiential knowledge of God lays the groundwork for understanding our identity.

CHAPTER 6

# Knowing Your Identity

ONE ORDINARY DAY, during my quiet time with God, I sat in His presence, eagerly awaiting to hear His voice. Shortly after, He uttered a single word: exotic. Naturally, my first thought was that He must be referring to my physical appearance. As an immigrant in America, I have grown accustomed to receiving comments and questions about my distinctive looks and features, so it seemed like the obvious interpretation. Surely, He must be talking about my big, beautiful eyes, my naturally tanned skin tone, and my unique mannerisms, right?

Yet, all jokes aside, I have learned over the years that when God speaks, it is essential to seek His deeper perspective rather than assigning my interpretation or jumping to conclusions based on my own understanding (a mistake I have made many times). After all, our encounters with God—whether through Scriptures, inner promptings, dreams, or visions—are invitations to engage in deeper conversations.

So, this time, I decided to ask for His interpretation. I looked up the word exotic in the Oxford Dictionary and found it defined as "originating in or characteristic of a distant foreign country." God then began to reveal to me that the foreign country symbolized the Kingdom of heaven—a spiritual realm where He reigns as King.

In calling me exotic, God was affirming and solidifying my identity as His child and a citizen of His Kingdom. He was reminding me that I am "other-worldly"—someone born of Him and originating from and embodying the essence of His Kingdom while living in this world. This is my identity–and it is yours too!

## YOUR IDENTITY REVEALED

Understanding our true identity holds profound significance in developing a wealth mindset. Without understanding and revelation of our identity, we fail to manifest its fruits, leading to unchanged behaviors and actions.

Our perceptions of the world are fundamentally shaped by how we view ourselves. Living in a fallen world where people constantly label us negatively, our experiences in life attempt to define us, and the enemy assigns false identities to us, *how can we truly discover who we are?*

Even beyond these external influences, we define ourselves often by our occupations (jobs and work titles), nationalities, racial or ethnic backgrounds, family roles and statuses (single, married, or parent), educational backgrounds, or even our affinities for favorite sports teams. While these elements serve as natural descriptors of our outward persona and explain unique expressions of our individuality, they fall short of fully capturing our *core* identity.

> **Our core identity originates from our union with Christ, as we are found in Him.**

Our true identity must be informed by God's perspective as our Creator. It emerges when we believe His truths about us and align our thoughts and perspectives to perceive ourselves through His lens, irrespective of external influences. It is only through this alignment of belief and perspective that real transformation occurs in our lives. As Kris Vallotton articulates it, "The way you see yourself has a profound impact on how you think, feel, and behave. Only when you see yourself the way God sees you will you live the life He's destined for you to live."[1]

**Intimate knowledge of Christ is a prerequisite to knowing ourselves because our lives are mirrored in Him; in beholding Him, we perceive ourselves.**

How convinced are you about who God says you are—His perspective of your identity? Are you allowing your outward reality (external circumstances) or current behavior (performance) to dictate your perception of your identity? Our beliefs about ourselves shape our character and trajectory in life as transformation begins from within. What we focus on—whether positive or negative—is amplified. By renewing our minds with God's truth, our emotions and behaviors naturally align with His design for us.

Our core identity originates from our union with Christ, as we are found in Him. Ephesians 1:11-12 (MSG) tells us "It's in Christ that we find out who we are and what we are living for." This signifies that He is both the Source of our identity and the perfect reflection of God's image in us!

Through faith in Christ, we were reborn of God, born of the Spirit. Primarily, we are spiritual beings with eternal substance or origin, inhabiting bodies and souls, not the reverse. Our spirit man (inner man) reflects our true nature. After all, we were recreated in the image and likeness of Christ at salvation. Thus, when the Father looks at us, He beholds us in Christ.

Understanding our true identity in Christ is predicated on knowing God and His nature (character). Intimate knowledge of Christ is a prerequisite to knowing ourselves because our lives are mirrored in Him; in beholding Him, we perceive ourselves.

"But we all, with unveiled face, beholding as in a mirror the glory of the Lord, are being transformed into the same image from glory to glory, just as by the Spirit of the Lord." (2 Corinthians 3:18, NKJV)

The more we see Him, the more we see ourselves. What is true of Him is equally true of us (1 John 2:7-8). Christ is our potential: "As he is, so are we in this world" (1 John 4:17, NKJV). Our existence is intertwined with His (Acts 17:28). Therefore, the deeper our knowledge of Him, the clearer our understanding of ourselves becomes!

"We know also that the Son of God has come and has given us understanding, so that we may know him who is true. And we are in him who is true by being in his Son Jesus Christ. He is the true God and eternal life." (1 John 5:20, NIV)

Hence, awakening to our true identity in Christ is crucial for operating with a wealth mindset. It is fundamental for experiencing true transformation and revealing Christ—His light and character—in the world around us. Through this awareness, we can display the Kingdom of God as a tangible reality here on earth. With confidence, we can pursue our dreams and purposes, unlocking our full potential while living above our circumstances. The enemy trembles in the presence of those who are grounded in their identity. Truly, the benefits are endless when we grasp the revelation of our true identity in Christ.

## THE TRUTH ABOUT YOUR NEW IDENTITY

Discovering the truth about our new identity is a transformative journey that uncovers the boundless possibilities it unlocks for our lives. In this section, we will examine five major aspects of our identity in Christ.

### 1. Child of God

Through the cross, Christ ushered in a new covenant of grace, enabling all who believe—even those once enemies of God—to be welcomed as His children. Receiving a new identity as a child of God stands as one of the gospel's most profound gifts (benefits). No longer are we orphans left to fend for ourselves; rather, we are embraced by a loving Father who will never leave nor forsake us. We are graciously adopted into God's family, bestowed with the esteemed titles of sons and daughters of the Most High.

> "And you did not receive the 'spirit of religious duty,' leading you back into the fear of never being good enough. But you have received the 'Spirit of full acceptance,' enfolding you into the family of God. And you will never feel orphaned, for as he rises up within us, our spirits join him in saying the words of tender affection, 'Beloved Father!' For the Holy Spirit makes God's fatherhood real to us as he whispers into our innermost being, **'You are God's beloved child!'**" (Rom. 8:15-16, TPT, emphasis added)

Understanding our identity as children of God extends beyond intellectual acknowledgment; it includes a deep-rooted belief and knowing at the core of our being. It involves comprehending our rights and privileges—the benefits bestowed upon us—as well as embracing the responsibility that accompanies our esteemed position and recognizing the authority and power we possess.

As children of God, we enjoy the privilege of being intimately known, unconditionally loved, and fully accepted. God is closely acquainted with every detail of our lives; nothing is hidden from Him or takes Him by surprise. He knows our likes and dislikes, strengths and weaknesses, our deepest desires, and even the complexities of our motives—both good and evil. He understands our struggles in life. He is keenly aware of our past, present, and future. Yet, despite it all, we are accepted and loved!

As beloved children, we have the benefit of experiencing and sharing in the same love the Father enjoys with Jesus. In His eyes, we are inseparable from Christ; we are securely hidden in Him. Regardless of our behavior, God adores and delights in us unconditionally.

"The Lord your God is in your midst, a mighty one who will save; he will rejoice over you with gladness; he will quiet you by his love; he will exult over you with loud singing." (Zephaniah 3:17, ESV)

Those convinced of their identity as His children are consistently nourished internally and are empowered by His love. They find rest in His unwavering love, even when they fail to receive love from others. He becomes their primary source of love, continuously replenishing their need for love (love tanks) as they abide in Him. While the love they receive from others is cherished as an additional blessing—the cherry on top—it is His love that becomes their foundation to love themselves and others.

As God's children, we are also deeply and wholly accepted. Those who are firmly established in this acceptance become secure in their interactions with God and others, understanding that external rejection or lack of acceptance does not define their worth. They approach life from a position of already being fully accepted rather than seeking validation from others. They recognize that they do not need to perform to earn others' approval. God becomes their primary source of acceptance, satisfying their need for affirmation and validation first and foremost, instead of depending on others for approval. Even amidst misunderstanding and mistreatment, they draw from the Source. Their sense of self-worth and confidence are firmly anchored in the boundless love and acceptance of the Father.

The mature sons of God also comprehend and exercise their authority and power in Christ. They understand that they share the same authority and power that Jesus had during His earthly ministry. Empowered by the Holy Spirit, children of God have the ability to overcome the world: "For everyone who has been born of God overcomes the world. And this is the victory that has overcome the world—our faith" (1 John 5:4, ESV).

They are equipped to defeat Satan, as affirmed in Luke 10:19 (NIV): "I have given you authority to trample on snakes and scorpions and to overcome all the power of the enemy; nothing will harm you."

Moreover, they reign over sin, as emphasized in Romans 6:14 (NIV): "For sin shall not be master over you, for you are not under law but under grace." (See also Romans 6:2 and 1 Peter 2:24). They are entrusted with the key to the Kingdom of heaven, being empowered to exercise their authority and bring its influence on earth: "'I will give you the keys of heaven's kingdom realm to forbid on earth that which is forbidden in heaven, and to release on earth that which is released in heaven'" (Matthew 16:19, TPT).

Those who are children are also heirs of God and joint heirs with Christ, sharing in the inheritances of the Kingdom and partaking in all the spiritual blessings. Sonship qualifies us for both the privileges and responsibilities of being an heir not just in the afterlife but also here and right now. We not only inherit Christ Himself—the true, ultimate reward—but also everything that He owns, granting us full access to His Kingdom, if we also share in His sufferings.

> **We not only inherit Christ Himself—the true, ultimate reward—but also everything that He owns, granting us full access to His Kingdom . . .**

"And since we are his true children, we qualify to share all his treasures, for indeed, we are heirs of God himself. And since we are joined to Christ, **we also inherit all that he is and all that he has.** We will experience being co-glorified with him provided that we accept his sufferings as our own." (Romans 8:17, TPT)

### Sonship and a Wealth Mindset

Believers with a wealth mindset exude confidence in their sonship. They possess an understanding of being deeply loved and fully accepted in Christ. In their interactions with others, they radiate this unwavering security in God's love and acceptance, confidently exercise their authority and power in Christ, and strategically leverage their position as heirs of the Kingdom. Even amidst hardships, when their identity is tested, they steadfastly remind themselves of their cherished sonship.

## 2. New Creations

One of the mysteries of the gospel is the unveiling of our new identity as new creations in Christ (2 Corinthians 5:17). Despite our familiarity with this Scripture, many of us have yet to fully grasp and internalize its truth. We have barely scratched the surface beyond simply memorizing and reciting it without fully embracing its profound revelations and implications. What is needed is a deep revelation of this truth, as it produces faith within us, empowering us to actualize and embody it in our daily lives.

When we accepted Christ, we underwent a spiritual rebirth. While our physical body remained unchanged, our inner being (our spirit man) was regenerated—born of God and the Spirit (John 3:3). Through the rebirth experience, the fullness of the Triune God—Father, Son, and Holy Spirit—came to dwell within us as believers. This new man is no longer *merely* human but altogether a new being. We are indeed a new breed, marked by new quality, new ability, and newness of nature—whether we realize it

> This union, the mystery of Christ in us, is what makes us a new creation and gives us a completely new identity.

or not. This inner transformation is what the Bible describes as the birth of a new creation.

Faith in Christ initiated our union with Him. This union, the mystery of Christ in us, is what makes us a new creation and gives us a completely new identity:

"My old identity has been co-crucified with Christ and no longer lives. And now the essence of this new life is no longer mine, for the Anointed One lives his life through me—we live in union as one! My new life is empowered by the faith of the Son of God who loves me so much that he gave himself for me, dispensing his life into mine." (Galatians 2:20, TPT)

Although the spiritual birth within us is invisible to the naked eye and transcends human comprehension, the truth remains: our old self died and was buried with Jesus, while our new self was resurrected to new life with Him.

> "'Or don't you know that all of us who were baptized into Christ Jesus were baptized into his death? We were therefore buried with him through baptism into death in order that, just as Christ was raised from the dead through the glory of the Father, we too may live a new life. For if we have been united with him in a death like his, we will certainly also be united with him in a resurrection like his.'" (Romans 6:3-5, NIV)

The old nature, which was in Adam, along with its lusts and sinful desires, has been utterly destroyed. In its place stands the new nature, which is found in Christ Jesus: the Last Adam.

### The New Nature of the New Creation

So, who is this new creation? What does he look like? The new man, who is recreated in Christ, does not emerge from our own striving, performance, or good deeds. Rather, it is the culmination of Christ's finished work on the cross—it is the grace of God! Perhaps the only "work" remaining for us to do is to align ourselves with this truth, wholeheartedly believe it, and walk in agreement with the reality of our new identity. If we endeavor to attain the qualities of the new creation on our own, we risk severing ourselves from grace.

The Bible teaches that the new man is fashioned after the image and likeness of God. We are His image-bearers. Ephesians 4:24 (ESV) commands us "to put on the new self, created after the likeness of God in true righteousness and holiness." Hence, our new nature mirrors the righteousness and holiness of God Himself. It also embodies qualities such as wholeness, kindness, gentleness, compassion, truthfulness, humility, and patience, all attributes of Christ Himself: "Put on then, as God's chosen ones, holy and beloved, compassionate hearts, kindness, humility, meekness, and patience" (Colossians 3:12, ESV).

Therefore, view yourselves as already clothed with your new identity as you would wear new lenses or glasses—it is who you already are in Christ, not who you strive to become. These qualities cannot be manufactured through human effort anyway. By recognizing your true identity, you find rest from striving. Our focus as the new creation should be on "being" rather than "doing," and through this being, the fruits naturally blossom and become evident in our lives.

**Your experiences do not dictate the truth; rather, the truth defines your experiences.**

John Crowder beautifully captures the essence of the new creation with these words: "The new you is happy, alive, and full of the wine of His love. The new you is full of faith. The new, True Self, is prosperous, bold, and overflowing with life, hope, peace, and fruitfulness. The new self is completely restored to childlike innocence and trust."[2]

Does it sound too good to be true? Surprisingly, it absolutely is true! Stop referring to your past or present experiences of who you have been to define who you are. Your experiences do not dictate the truth; rather, the truth defines your experiences. Even in moments when you feel disconnected from or find yourself out of alignment with your true identity, remind yourself of who you are in Christ.

Remember, your old self is no longer who you are:

"Put off your old self, which belongs to your former manner of life and is corrupt through deceitful desires, and [instead] **to be renewed in the spirit of your minds,** and to put on the new self." (Ephesians 4:22-24, ESV)

Rather than attempting to fix yourself, simply rest in what Christ has already made you to be. Meditate on the truth of your new identity. Be continually renewed, having a fresh, untainted attitude about your new self. The more you reaffirm your identity in Christ, the more your behavior will naturally align with your true self.

### Sin and the New Creation

How should we view sin in light of this newfound identity?

While many Christians understand sin as breaking God's moral code or transgressing the law, this definition barely scratches the surface. It fails to address the source, or the root cause, of sin. Upon deeper reflection, I have come to realize that sin is essentially a distortion of one's identity, resulting in wrong (erroneous) beliefs and actions. The Holy Spirit revealed to me that every manifestation of sin can be traced back to a flawed perception of one's identity. In essence, sin is an identity crisis.

> **Sin is essentially a distortion of one's identity, resulting in wrong (erroneous) beliefs and actions.**

Sin is not limited to what we do; it is being out of alignment with our true nature in Christ. As Francois Du Toit aptly describes it, sin is "a mistaken identity, a perversion from our true design. It's buying into the identity of another, e.g., addict, liar, gossip."[3] Furthermore, he emphasizes that sin represents separation from God and from His identity, which has now become ours in Christ.

Consider the Scripture below in different translations:

> **Every manifestation of sin can be traced back to a flawed perception of one's identity . . . Sin is an identity crisis.**

"My dear children, I write this to you **so that you will not sin.** But if anybody does sin, we have an advocate with the Father—Jesus Christ, the Righteous One." (1 John 2:1, NIV, emphasis added)

"My darling little children, the reason that I write these things to you is **so that you will not believe a lie about yourselves!** If anyone does believe a distorted image to be their reality, we have Jesus Christ who defines our likeness face to face with the Father!" (1 John 2:1, The Mirror, emphasis added)

As The Mirror translation states above, sin is believing a lie about ourselves, a lie spoken over us by either the enemy or by the world. Sin entails adopting a false identity that God never gave us or intended for us. Therefore, as new creations in Christ, let us deliberately choose to believe what God declares about us.

So, do you recognize sin as a distortion of your perceived identity in Christ, contrary to your true nature, and something you have already died to? Or do you still view sin as an unavoidable aspect of our existence in a fallen world, and something you tolerate or wrestle down in a battle with the flesh until Jesus' return?

While some may be inclined to adopt the latter mindset solely based on their experiences, the word of God encourages us to embrace a different perspective:

> "Our old man was crucified with Him, that the body of sin might be done away with, that we should no longer be slaves of sin. For he who has died has been freed from sin." (Romans 6:6-7, NKJV)

> "When he [Jesus] died, **he died once to break the power of sin**. But now that he lives, he lives for the glory of God. **So you also should consider yourselves to be dead to the power of sin and alive to God through Christ Jesus**." (Romans 6:10-11, NLT, emphasis added)

Believers with this mindset are convinced of their union with Christ and believe that Jesus has already dealt with and abolished sin—the entirety or body of sin. They trust that whatever is true for Christ is true for them.

**Faith precedes manifestation; trust your new identity to manifest reality through your belief.**

Faith precedes manifestation; trust your new identity to manifest reality through your belief. Remember, we do not automatically behave out of our true identity but out of our understanding of our identity. In the brilliant spoken words of C.S. Lewis:

> "You are what you believe. If you believe you are still a sinner, you will manifest sin. If you believe you are the

righteousness of God in Christ Jesus, then you are going to manifest righteousness. Believe you are holy and you will manifest holy. That is who you really are."[4]

Be cautioned here: this view does not advocate for sinless perfection, which suggests that it is impossible to sin. It is certainly against righteousness through works, which stands in stark contrast to sinless perfection and is demonstrated by the need to "kill the flesh," also known as self-righteousness. However, there exists a God-given righteousness that comes through faith:

"Therefore no one will be declared righteous in his sight by observing the law; rather, through the law we become conscious of sin. But, now a righteousness from God, apart from the law, has been made known, to which the law and prophets testify. This righteousness from God comes through faith in Jesus Christ to all who believe." (Romans 3:20-21, NIV)

### New Creation and a Wealth Mindset

Believers with a wealth mindset understand their true identity as new creations. They perceive themselves through the lens of how God sees them—in Christ. They set their gaze on Christ as the Source and foundation of their identity as they mirror His character. Rather than focusing on their weaknesses and failures—their experiences—they focus their thoughts on the realities of the new man (Colossians 3:1-3).

They possess righteousness consciousness rather than sin consciousness, viewing themselves as saints rather than sinners. Their union with Christ allows them to adopt His nature as their own—joy, peace, love, holiness, and prosperity. Through the sharpening of their spiritual senses, they recognize any distortion in their thoughts or actions, prompting them to quick repentance and the renewal of their minds as they walk in step with the Holy Spirit.

### 3. Royalty

The rebirth experience that sealed our sonship also established our identity as royalty—sons and daughters of the King. We are not only royalty by birth but also by marriage—united to King Jesus Himself. In 1 Peter 2:9 (ESV), Scripture solidifies our identity, declaring, "You are a chosen race, a **royal priesthood,** a holy nation, a people for his own possession, that you may proclaim the excellencies of him who called you out of darkness into his marvelous light" (emphasis added).

> **We are not only royalty by birth but also by marriage—united to King Jesus Himself.**

In his book *Kingdom Principles,* Dr. Myles Munroe eloquently portrays our identity as royals within the grand narrative of God's eternal plan:

> "The Bible is about a King, a Kingdom, and a royal family of children...its story and message are about the desire of a King to extend His Kingdom to new territories through His royal family."

In this context, as royalty, we represent the King and His Kingdom here on earth. We bring its culture and realities to the world around us. Our service and allegiance to the King extends beyond the confines of church walls and into our respective spheres of influence, including the marketplace.

Our status and title were instantly elevated to regality when "God raised us up with Christ and seated us with him in the heavenly realms in Christ Jesus" (Ephesians 2:6, NIV). In the spiritual realm, we enjoy the privilege of being seated at the right hand of the Father in His throne room in Christ Jesus, even as we live in the natural world. Through our position in Christ, seated in this place of honor and favor, we gain access to an elevated perspective, viewing all things and situations through His eyes.

Our regal status also automatically qualifies us to a position of power and authority, asserting our original mandate to exercise dominion over the earth from heaven and to reign over the world system—to live about it and not succumb to its demands.

Our newfound position also carries the responsibility of service. As royals who also function as priests, we minister to both God and people. Bill Johnson insightfully explains the connection: "Royalty is my identity. Servanthood is my assignment. Intimacy with God is my life source."[5] Genuine service is born out of a secure understanding of our identity in Christ, not from a fear of God's judgment, obligation, or as a transaction for blessings.

> "For you did not receive the spirit of slavery to fall back into fear, but you have received the Spirit of adoption as sons, by whom we cry, 'Abba! Father!'" (Romans 8:14-15, ESV)

Our royalty, rather than restricting us, grounds us for service: "Therefore you are no longer a slave (bond-servant), but a son; and if a son, then also an heir through [the gracious act of] God [through Christ]" (Galatians 4:7, AMP).

When reflecting on human history and earthly kingdoms, royalty is often associated with being served rather than serving, and the concept of royalty and servitude may appear contradictory. However, this is the culture of God's Kingdom, modeled after Jesus Himself, the Servant King.

Lastly, our royalty entitles us to enjoy abundant provisions from the King. Dr. Myles Munroe beautifully articulates it: "Once we are under the rule of this gracious, merciful, benevolent, loving, caring King, He takes personal responsibility for us, not as servants or serfs, but as family and royal children."[6] True royals in Christ are confident in the kindhearted and good-natured King, focusing on the Kingdom and their relationship with Him rather than on their personal needs (Matthew 6:33).

Even in difficult times, they trust their King (Father) to meet all their needs. As heirs and joint-heirs of the Kingdom with Christ, they understand they have access to the King's abundance, as God's Kingdom knows no lack. Their lavish provision also results in abundant generosity toward those in need, inspired by the benevolent nature of their King. Compelled by His goodness, they work diligently to fulfill their dreams and visions, aiming to expand His Kingdom and spread His fame.

### Royalty and a Wealth Mindset

Believers with a wealth mindset are anchored in their identity as royalty in Christ. They think, decide, and behave like nobility in the Kingdom, embodying a spirit of excellence. Their high sense of worth in Christ and self-respect exudes infectious confidence, which may occasionally be misconstrued as overconfidence or pride. They lead lives of integrity, demonstrating resolute loyalty to their King. Their words and actions are characterized by courage and grace. Their lives are marked by generosity and servanthood. Above all, they are Kingdom-minded.

## 4. Citizens of the Kingdom

Another aspect of our identity that we instantly received at salvation was citizenship in the Kingdom of God: "But we are citizens of heaven, where the Lord Jesus Christ lives. And we are eagerly waiting for him to return as our Savior" (Philippians 3:20, NLT). Despite having dual citizenship in both heaven and earth, we are not defined by the earthly realm, as our true allegiance lies with the Kingdom of God. We were rescued from the kingdom of darkness into the Kingdom of light, whose King is Jesus (Colossians 1:12-13).

> As citizens, we serve as gateways or portals between heaven and earth, carrying within us the Kingdom of heaven. Indeed, we are carriers of God Himself.

Our citizenship qualifies us to be ambassadors of the Kingdom. Just as there are physical embassies and ambassadors representing different nations and governments within a host country, we also serve as representatives of heaven's government on earth. Our primary mission as citizens and ambassadors is to introduce others to the King and His Kingdom: "Now then, we are ambassadors for Christ, as though God were pleading through us: we implore you on Christ's behalf, be reconciled to God" (2 Corinthians 5:20, NKJV). As citizens, we serve as gateways or portals between heaven and earth, carrying within us the Kingdom of heaven. Indeed, we are carriers of God Himself.

Many Christians fail to grasp that our salvation is not just for personal redemption but also for the grander purpose of "For King and Kingdom." Without a clear understanding of the Kingdom's broader vision, many of us overlook the deeper significance of our salvation. This limited high-level understanding of the Kingdom has led us to fall short of *accurately* representing the benevolent King.

The world is yearning for a savior, often unaware of their own hunger. Perhaps if we intimately knew the King and accurately represented Him, people would be attracted to Him—sometimes even without our words, but by simply showing up in our authentic identity. If through us, they can take a glimpse of the beauty and the majesty of the King, His love and goodness, and the magnificence of His Kingdom, they cannot help but flock to His Kingdom. The good news of the Kingdom spread like wildfire during the early church period: "The Law and the Prophets were proclaimed until John. Since that time, the good news of the kingdom of God is being preached, and everyone is forcing his way into it" (Luke 16:16, NIV, emphasis added). I cannot help but wonder if our religiosity and righteousness policing have become stumbling blocks, hindering people from eagerly embracing the Kingdom simply because we have failed to exemplify what it truly means to be good citizens and ambassadors of the Kingdom.

> If through us, they can take a glimpse of the beauty and the majesty of the King, His love and goodness, and the magnificence of His Kingdom, they cannot help but flock to His Kingdom.

Citizenship in affluent and highly developed nations such as America is greatly coveted; people from around the world would go to great lengths to immigrate and secure citizenship due to the promise of a better life. It is not surprising that these nations' governments vigorously defend the right of citizenship, recognizing the immense power and influence it holds. Similarly, if the world understood the desirability of the Kingdom, they would swarm to it.

However, unlike citizenship in first-world nations, citizenship in this invisible yet very real Kingdom is open and freely available to all who accept Christ. Just because it is free does not diminish its value or significance. In fact, the King Himself paid the ultimate and greatest price ever by shedding His blood and giving His life away on the cross. Citizenship in this Kingdom represents the highest of the high!

Finally, as citizens, we enjoy the privilege of sharing in the abundance of the Kingdom of God. Dr. Myles Munroe beautifully explains the value of citizens to their King:

"In a kingdom, the concept of 'commonwealth' is also very important, and the word correctly describes the nature of the relationship the king has with his citizens and subjects. The wealth in a kingdom is common. Therefore, in a true ideal kingdom there is no discrimination or distinction between the rich and the poor, for in such a kingdom all citizens have equal access to kingdom wealth and resources provided by the benevolent king. In essence, the King's interest is the welfare of the Kingdom and everything in it."[7]

### Citizenship and a Wealth Mindset

Believers with a wealth mindset understand their identity as citizens and their unique position as the interface between heaven and earth. They accurately represent the King, making Him irresistible to the world. They become a living display of the King's goodness and magnificence, attracting others to His Kingdom.

## 5. The Bride of Christ

As if all of the above were not enough, we also became the bride of Christ when we said "yes" to Him. Together with the entire body of Christ, we entered into an eternal marital union with Him. In Hosea 2:19 (NKJV), God declares, "I will betroth you to Me forever."

By His life, death, resurrection, and ascension, Jesus became the perfect embodiment of the loving Bridegroom and faithful Husband. Through our marital union with the Lamb, we can experience love in its purest and most innocent form—asexual, yet deeply intimate. We are His beloved!

In Song of Solomon, a poetic and symbolic depiction (allegory) of the love between Christ and His bride, the beloved (representing the church) declares her love: "My lover is mine and I am his" (Song of Solomon 2:16, NLT). In doing so, she acknowledges and celebrates her longing for intimacy with God, pointing to her ultimate desire of being united with Him. As His bride, we possess the marriage right of experiencing this deep, intimate love with Christ, which satisfies like no other!

> **Christ's love for the ekklēsia is great; He sacrificed Himself for her, made her holy, cleansing her by His word, and continues to nourish and cherish her.**

Additionally, we are privileged to embark on a life-long journey of exploring and discovering the mystery of our oneness with Christ—its multifaceted expressions and benefits. As the Scriptures affirm, "'A man leaves his father and mother and is joined to his wife, and the two are united into one.' This is a great mystery, but it is an illustration of the way Christ and the church are one" (Ephesians 5:31-32, NLT). Indeed, Christ's love for the ekklēsia (Greek for "church") is great; He sacrificed Himself for her (Ephesians 5:25), made her holy, cleansing her by His word (v. 26), and continues to nourish and cherish her (v. 29).

When we are united with God in marriage, the possibilities are limitless! Charles Spurgeon powerfully expressed this eternal marriage between Christ and the Church: "On earth He exercises towards her all the affectionate offices of Husband. He makes rich provisions for her wants, pays all her debts, allows her to assume His name, and to share in all His wealth. Nor will He ever act otherwise to her."[8]

### The Bride of Christ and a Wealth Mindset

Believers with a wealth mindset realize their oneness with Christ as His bride. They find satisfaction and sustenance for life through their intimacy with the Bridegroom, drinking deeply of His love. They rest in the care and provision of Christ, their loving and faithful Husband, who attends to their spiritual, emotional, physical, and financial needs. They understand that living in fear and worry is a contradiction as well as an insult to their identity as the beloved of Christ.

As we conclude this chapter, I urge you once more to refocus and fix your gaze on the cross, where Christ accomplished everything necessary to grant you a new identity. Do not allow yourself to be disoriented by the opinions of others or your past and present experiences to find your true self. Instead, shed your former self by being renewed in the spirit of your mind to fully embrace your new identity. Remind yourself regularly and reaffirm who you are in Christ! Meditate on it, declare it, sing it—let it sink in!

John Crowder says it this way: "Christian growth and maturity is about discovering our true identity and not becoming it."[9] In other words, we must simply continually awaken to the truth of our new identity, agree, and rest in that truth. The truth we believe will naturally manifest in our lives without the need for striving and performance. As they say, how can you manifest if you do not believe, and how can you believe if you have not heard? Now, you cannot say you have not heard!

In the upcoming chapter, we will explore the concept of giving, which is a significant aspect of expressing our new identity in Christ and displaying a wealth mindset. We will look at giving from a fresh perspective, reframing our understanding of it while empowering us to fully embody a wealth mindset.

## CHAPTER 7

# Giving Reframed

"God is more concerned with the motive behind the action
than the action itself. Giving with a wrong heart is of
no benefit—it is just attempted bribery."

JAMES BAKER[1]

GIVING IS ONE of the most powerful and effective ways to cultivate a wealth mindset and simultaneously break free from a poverty mentality. It disrupts existing patterns of scarcity thinking while making way for abundant thinking, especially when done in larger or sacrificial amounts and with repetition. When we give more, we develop a level of trust in and dependence on God that shifts our focus from what we lack to what we can contribute, thereby altering our perspective from lack to abundance.

While this holds true spiritually, science also validates this reality. Neuroscientists affirm that our habits and behaviors (such as giving) produce new neural pathways in the brain, which are responsible for creating our memories and enabling new learning and thinking patterns. Through repetition, these newly formed neural pathways become stronger, forging a pathway for new mindsets that eventually become established. Conversely, the principle also holds true: adopting new thinking patterns forms new neural pathways in the brain, serving as the foundation for acquired behaviors that become the new norm. Thus, abundant thinking leads to abundant giving: "For as he [man] thinks in his heart, so is he" (Proverbs 23:7, NKJV).

> **Giving reflects the condition of our heart, which is revealed through the things we treasure the most. It serves as a test of the authenticity of our faith, proving our trust in God's goodness and provision.**

Giving demonstrates our readiness to share our resources—money, time, gifts, and knowledge—with others. Unlike other behaviors, giving reflects the condition of our heart, which is revealed through the things we treasure the most (Matthew 6:21). It serves as a test of the authenticity of our faith, proving our trust in God's goodness and provision. In the realm of finances, it can be likened to a litmus test indicating whether we have the love of money or not.

Therefore, it is crucial to renew our minds (or create new neural pathways) regarding giving. Let's explore some powerful truths to better understand what genuine giving is—the reasons behind our giving and how we should approach it.

## GIVING PLEASES GOD

First and foremost, we give because it pleases God. Scripture reminds us not to "forget to do good and to share with others, for with such sacrifices God is pleased" (Hebrews 13:16, NIV). It gives Him pleasure, perhaps because we are never more like

Him than when we give; giving is an expression of His character, His love language. When we give, we reflect His image to the world, making Him tangible to others. After all, He gave His most prized possession—His one and only Son—as a gift. Along with Jesus Christ, He freely gave us all other things, not withholding anything (Romans 8:32).

## GIVING IS AN EXPRESSION OF LOVE

Genuine giving is a choice (an act of our will), a willingness to extend ourselves in service to another. True generosity is selfless; it never seeks to benefit itself. It can only be motivated by empathy to help a person in need, to seek a higher good for a group, or simply to bless another.

It is possible to give, even in excess, without love. Victor Hugo succinctly captures this notion: "You can give without loving, but you can never love without giving."[2] Love is not measured by actions alone; our motives determine what is considered loving. The outward expression of our giving must be aligned with our motives, the inward positioning.

In a letter to the Corinthian Church, the Apostle Paul vividly explains this truth: "If I give all my possessions to feed the poor, and if I surrender my body to be burned, but do not have love, it does me no good at all" (1 Corinthians 13:3, AMP). We can even sacrifice our lives for others and yet not have love. What a waste!

So, what motives disqualify our giving from being an expression of genuine, selfless love? Giving driven by obligation, whether perceived as a sense of religious duty, commitment, or a sense of indebtedness for a service or favor, falls short of true generosity. Similarly, giving under pressure or compulsion lacks the authenticity of heartfelt generosity (2 Corinthians 9:7). When giving is motivated by a desire for praise or admiration from others (Matthew 6:1-4), or is done with the expectation of a return—such as securing future favors through manipulation (transactional giving) (Luke 6:35)—it deviates from the essence of genuine giving.

Additionally, giving to gain approval or acceptance, to be liked or valued by others, or as a means to earn God's love or favor are motivations that undermine the purity of selfless giving. Surprise, surprise! All of these motives are characteristics that can be traced back to a poverty mindset.

Conversely, giving spurred by love is done willingly and wholeheartedly (1 Chronicles 29:9). It is cheerful, motivated by the joy of giving to others. It is free from the expectation of a return or benefit and is not self-serving. It gives secretly without a desire to be rewarded for good deeds (Matthew 6:3). More importantly, it extends itself generously and even sacrificially—all characteristics of a wealth mindset!

Therefore, when we give, let us examine our hearts frequently to make sure our motives are pure and others-focused, for we have a Father who sees in secret and rewards openly.

## GIVING ACKNOWLEDGES GOD AS THE SOURCE

Giving recognizes God as the ultimate Source of all our resources—money, time, and skills. It highlights the sovereignty of God as the giver of all blessings and provisions. A person with a wealth mindset realizes that there is an unlimited supply of resources in God (the Kingdom) and therefore gives generously without any fear of running out.

King David exhibits this profound understanding during the collection of resources for the building of the temple in Jerusalem. He prayed, "Everything comes from you, and we have given you only what comes from your hand" (1 Chronicles 29:14, NIV). David acknowledged that even our most generous giving is only a portion of what God has already given us from His abundant supply. Our act of giving (to others) is, in itself, a return to God. We are simply returning a portion of what God has entrusted to us as good stewards.

Our giving demonstrates to others our great stewardship based on our understanding of the Source and our reliance on Him for our provision.

## GIVING CAN BE SACRIFICIAL

When we recognize that everything ultimately originates from God and His abundant supply, it motivates cheerful, sacrificial giving. There is always more from where it comes!

The author of Hebrews encourages believers to make two kinds of sacrifices: the sacrifice of praise and the sacrifice of giving.

> "Therefore, let us offer through Jesus a continual sacrifice of praise to God, proclaiming our allegiance to his name. And don't forget to do good and to share with those in need. These are the sacrifices that please God." (Hebrews 13:15-16, NLT)

Allow me to explain the analogy between the two. Praising God during times of ease and blessing, when life is going well, is a simple task that many can accomplish. However, when faced with hardships and struggles, praising God becomes painful and challenging, and only a few summon the strength and faith to engage in it. Demonstrating such praise demands spiritual maturity and a steadfast heart that can look beyond difficulties to express gratitude and praise to God, regardless of circumstances. It is the praises offered in these challenging times that become truly sacrificial and bring the greatest delight to God.

Similarly, giving is relatively easy when we are in times of abundance and surplus beyond our needs, requiring minimal faith. When we experience lack (perceived or real) and struggle to make ends meet, yet still give when God prompts us, it is sacrificial; it is next-level giving. Giving in such circumstances is challenging and requires mature faith and obedience to overlook our needs and meet the needs of others. However, our reward is proportionately greater, as God is not indebted to anyone.

Paul testifies and brags about the churches in Macedonia who, "in the midst of a very severe trial, their overflowing joy and their extreme poverty welled up in rich generosity...They gave as much as they were able, and even beyond their ability" (2 Corinthians 8:2-6, NIV, emphasis added). Giving according to our ability is noble, but beyond our ability is divine or

> Giving according to our ability is noble, but beyond our ability is divine or God-like!

God-like! Generosity of such magnitude is characteristic of individuals who possess the mind of Christ (a wealth mindset). Paul urges Titus to establish this generous, grace-empowered, sacrificial giving as the standard to be replicated and embraced in the Corinthian Church and, by extension, by all New Testament believers.

## GIVING IS LEARNED (GIVING GROWS)

The moment we are reborn of the Spirit, our new man, recreated after the image and nature of God, has a new, built-in desire to give because it is God's nature to give. However, this desire needs to be nurtured and acted upon. As we learn to give more and more, the appetite to give develops in us. As we grow in intimacy with God, learning to hear His voice and obeying

His leading to give, we mature in the act of giving. It becomes second nature. We learn to give in abundance (quantity) with greater frequency and even sacrificially or beyond our ability. Just as we grow and mature in all areas of spiritual life, we also grow in generosity:

> "But since you excel in everything—in faith, in speech, in knowledge, in complete earnestness and in the love we have kindled in you—see that you also excel in this grace of giving." (2 Corinthians 8:7, NIV)

## GIVING BRINGS PROSPERITY

According to the conventional worldview, giving is primarily seen through a financial lens—defined by gain or loss—and is often transactional. It is not perceived as a gain unless an expected return is anticipated. Otherwise, giving is viewed as a reduction of resources—one ends up with fewer resources than they originally had. Simple math! However, giving in the Kingdom is counter-intuitive. When we give with a pure motive, we *always* gain, which is a stark contrast to the worldly perspective. We end up with more than we originally had, yet the return may not always come in the form, quantity, or time period it was given in the spiritual realm.

> Giving plays a critical role in living (and staying) in God's abundant economy.

Giving, in this context, opens the door to prosperity, bringing about a multiplication of blessings in all areas of life. It plays a critical role in living (and staying) in God's abundant economy. In 2 Corinthians 9:6-8, Scripture affirms that those who give generously will be blessed abundantly, emphasizing the reciprocity nature of giving. Biblical generosity leads to prosperity, bringing refreshment to both the giver and the recipient. In short, giving attracts abundance! Conversely, withholding has the opposite effect; it attracts lack (Proverbs 11:24-25)!

> **Giving attracts abundance! Conversely, withholding has the opposite effect; it attracts lack!**

Nevertheless, the emphasis always rests on the attitude of the heart when giving. It always points to our motives. We are called to give without the expectation of getting, for God cannot be deceived or manipulated. We give because love compels us to refresh and restore others, to see the Kingdom advance in all spheres, and to spread the gospel of Jesus Christ. We give simply because we love God!

## GIVING IS GRATITUDE AND WORSHIP

Giving is a language of gratitude toward God, a means of expressing our thanksgiving for His abundant provision in our lives. The acknowledgment that we have freely received from God through His grace in itself generates a heart filled with gratitude, which naturally overflows with generosity. Essentially, we freely give because we have freely received. This act of giving goes beyond a simple gesture; it transforms into an act of worship, a profound way to honor and glorify God for His many blessings.

The act of giving not only reflects gratitude by the giver but also elicits a response of thanksgiving in the receiver:

> "You will be enriched in every way so that you may be generous, and this generosity, administered through us, is producing thanksgiving to God from those who benefit." (2 Corinthians 9:11, AMP)

In this dynamic, the concepts of giving, gratitude, and worship are intertwined, creating a profound connection between the giver, the receiver, and God.

## GIVING IS A SOURCE OF JOY

The act of giving is intricately linked to the joy derived from selflessly contributing to the well-being of others and supporting God's work. Perhaps one of the most significant blessings of giving is the profound sense of satisfaction and joy it creates in the heart of the giver. It is no wonder that givers are often regarded as the happiest people on earth! If you want to multiply your joy, increase your giving—not out of obligation or for self-serving motives but out of genuine desire and sincerity.

Undoubtedly, giving serves as the antidote to sadness or depression. Jesus truly understood the secret of giving when He stated, "'It is more blessed [and brings greater joy] to give than to receive'" (Acts 20:35, AMP). This statement highlights the idea that there is a special blessing and joy that comes from giving, surpassing the satisfaction that comes from receiving alone.

## GIVING IS AN ACT OF FAITH

True giving is a spiritual act rooted in faith. It is an expression of faith in God's abundant provision and a demonstration of trust in His promises. It requires trust in God's goodness to care for our needs and the allocation of our resources to meet the needs of others.

Giving requires eyes of faith that see beyond the seen and scarce world's economy into the invisible

> **Giving requires eyes of faith that see beyond the seen and scarce world's economy into the invisible and abundant economy of God's Kingdom.**

and abundant economy of God's Kingdom. It involves aligning our resources to match His Kingdom's values and principles and participating in its purposes.

It especially requires greater faith to give sacrificially out of one's scarcity. Remember the widow and her mite! In this story, Jesus zooms in and marvels at this poor widow who put two small copper coins, worth only a fraction of a penny—all she had—into the temple treasury when others were giving in large amounts out of their wealth (Mark 12:41-44). Although not mentioned explicitly, I believe Jesus commended her faith for sacrificially giving despite the small monetary value she could offer.

## GIVING LED BY THE SPIRIT

In the new covenant of grace, those who are led by the Spirit of God are the ones recognized as the children of God (Romans 8:14). This is what marks the mature sons of God! They are attuned to the guidance and prompting of the Holy Spirit in all areas of their lives. Giving is no different! Our giving should also be led by the Holy Spirit. While there is nothing wrong with habitual giving driven by personal initiative, bountiful fruit comes when our giving is Spirit-led.

> In Spirit-led giving, we willingly surrender ourselves and our resources to His Lordship.

In Spirit-led giving, we willingly surrender ourselves and our resources to His Lordship. Being Spirit-led requires remaining sensitive to His prompting to give. Like a branch connected to the vine (source) at all times, we should also stay continuously attuned to His voice, which can be discerned through prayer, meditation, a strong desire, or a sense of conviction.

At times, the Holy Spirit may bring a person, an organization, or a cause to mind and move us to give financially.

Alternatively, He might expose us to a situation or need, stirring within us a desire and compassion to respond through giving. Sometimes, He may guide us by specifying the exact amount to give and, at other times, give us the freedom to decide the amount. At times, He might counsel refraining from meeting a seemingly real need, revealing the hidden motives of manipulation in the person seeking assistance. Alternatively, He may advise against giving to prevent us from intervening in His divine process of building trust and faith in the individual seeking aid. Whatever the case, trust and follow His leading!

If there is a lack of peace in your heart regarding your desire to give, ask the Holy Spirit for confirmation. However, do not confuse this with your personal unease about giving, creating every excuse in your heart for why not to give.

Giving led by the Spirit is a personal and relational journey. Like any spiritual act, it requires a close relationship with God, a listening heart, and a willingness to be obedient to His leading.

## NON-MONETARY GIVING

Despite what comes to mind first, giving is not limited to finances. Non-monetary forms of giving include using our time, gifts, talents, emotions, and energy in service to others. While there is an overlap between the different forms of giving, let's take a closer look individually.

One way we engage in non-monetary giving is through the investment of our time in others. This may take the form of actively listening to others in their time of need and providing our physical presence to comfort them. It may also take the form of offering encouragement and emotional support (a kind word or uplifting someone's spirit), as encouraged in 1 Thessalonians 5:11 (NIV): "Therefore encourage one

another and build each other up, just as in fact you are doing."
Additionally, we can invest our time in prayer, interceding for
others, and lifting up their needs, concerns, and well-being
before God: "And pray in the Spirit on all occasions with all
kinds of prayers and requests. With this in mind, be alert and
always keep on praying for all the Lord's people" (Ephesians
6:18, NIV). Hesitation to invest time and effort in relationships, fearing that it is a drain on our limited time may be a
manifestation of a poverty mindset. A wealth mindset invests
time in at least a few meaningful relationships.

Another form of non-monetary giving involves sharing our
knowledge, wisdom, and understanding with others, spanning
from God's word to any field of expertise in any area of life.
Paul celebrates the church in Rome by writing, "I myself am
satisfied about you, my brothers, that you yourselves are full
of goodness, filled with all knowledge and able to instruct
one another" (Romans 15:14, ESV). Likewise, he exhorts the
Colossians to "let the word of Christ dwell in you richly, teaching and admonishing one another in all wisdom" (Colossians
3:16 ESV). Any reluctance to share knowledge or information,
driven by the belief that others' success diminishes personal
opportunities, is an expression of a scarcity mindset. This
mindset also reveals itself by the constant fostering of compe-
tition over collaboration, creating an environment of rivalry
rather than cooperation and collective growth.

Moreover, non-monetary giving extends to serving others
through our diverse gifts, talents, and abilities—whether "natural" or spiritual gifts—"Each of you should use whatever gift
you have received to serve others, as faithful stewards of God's
grace in its various forms" (1 Peter 4:10, NIV). The Bible lists
several spiritual gifts, such as administration, discernment,
exhortation, faith, healing, hospitality, mercy, and prophecy.

Exercising any one of your gifts is a non-monetary form of giving that expresses love and care for others. Likewise, we can share our natural gifts in business, technology, art, and more through volunteering or mentorship.

Lastly, our non-monetary giving can be expressed through emotions. Strange, I know! Forgiveness, which is both an emotion and decision, is considered an example of non-monetary giving that involves letting go of resentment and extending grace and mercy to others (Colossians 3:13). Paul in his epistle emphasizes the importance of clothing ourselves with these emotions: "Therefore, as God's chosen people, holy and dearly loved, clothe yourselves with **compassion, kindness, humility, gentleness, and patience**" (Colossians 3:12, NIV, emphasis added). Any display of these sound and solid characters, or showing emotional maturity, are forms of non-monetary giving that reflect God's love through our emotions.

## GIVING VERSUS TITHING

Many in the church believe that God's command on tithing, a practice of giving a tenth of one's income as outlined to the Israelites in the Old Testament, remains applicable to the church today. On the contrary, others believe and advocate for grace-based, voluntary giving as the new standard for believers in the New Testament, as one who is under grace and not the law (where grace supersedes the law). Perhaps you find yourself navigating between these views, ascribing to certain aspects of both.

While both views have their own merits, the pivotal question revolves around the nature of our giving, its consistency, and the purity of our motives. Giving, fundamentally, is a matter of the heart. If you align with the tithing view and adhere to its practices, consider whether your tithing stems from obligation and adherence to a rigid, legalistic requirement as in the Old Testament or if it is led by the Spirit and motivated by love for God and others. Are you tithing as one under the law or as one under grace? It would be superior to believe and act on the far greater principles of grace, faith, and love. As New Testament believers, if God calls us to give generously, then tithing should be viewed as the bare minimum!

Conversely, if you embrace the grace-based giving view, reflect on whether you are giving generously, even sacrificially. Does your decision not to tithe serve as an excuse for irregular and inconsistent giving? When was the last time you gave? Those who tithe, at the very least, maintain a practice of giving regularly and consistently.

## LACK AS A CATALYST FOR GIVING

Sometimes, a giving attitude is formed in a person during seasons of lack. For those with surrendered hearts, encountering moments of lack can cultivate empathy and compassion toward the poor and those who are in need. Understanding others' struggles and pain can often seem elusive unless we navigate similar experiences ourselves. People with limited exposure to challenges or those who endure lack without allowing God to work within their hearts may become judgmental, dismissing others' struggles and attributing them to laziness.

This reflection brings to mind a story from many years ago about a notorious French queen who callously uttered the phrase "Qu'ils mangent de la brioche" ("Let them eat cake or brioche") during the tumultuous era of the French Revolution. Confronted with the alarming news of a bread shortage due to poor crop yields and a rodent infestation, the starving French population sought relief. In response to their plight, she heartlessly declared, "Let them eat cake!" This dismissive statement highlighted her arrogance and profound disconnect from the struggles of her subjects, as cake was a luxury item significantly more expensive than the staple food, bread.

Her insensitivity and obliviousness to the dire circumstances of the people contributed to her transformation into a despised symbol of the monarchy. The callousness embedded in her words became a catalyst for the resentment that fueled the flames of the French Revolution.

This historical episode vividly illustrates the importance of experiencing seasons of struggle and suffering that create in us God-like characters of empathy, compassion, and kindness as opposed to fostering judgment and arrogance. Indeed, empathy and compassion cultivate a generous heart within us.

In closing this chapter, I leave you with this thought. The act of giving is a powerful and effective method to shift our mindsets—breaking free from the chains of poverty thinking while paving the way for a mindset rooted in abundance. How we view and approach giving is indicative of our mindset, of how we perceive and trust God, and of how we view money. It is a tangible way for us to reflect His image in the world. Therefore, renewing our minds with the truth of biblical giving becomes crucial to bringing about real transformation in us. As we move forward, the upcoming chapter will further fuel our desire for giving as we explore the truth associated with money, a significant form of giving.

## CHAPTER 8

# Rethinking Money

"God is the Source of your wealth. You are the cause. Money is
just the side effect of your mindset and habits."

JAMES BAKER[1]

I COULD NOT start with a more fitting quote to illustrate the
dynamics and relationship among the key elements in the true
wealth equation from a Kingdom perspective—God, man, a
wealth mindset (habits), and money. Our mindsets and habits
must be shaped by Kingdom values to produce true wealth.
While God is the Source of true wealth, it is imperative that we
actively engage with Him to renew our minds and participate
in meaningful work where He places us.

Money, as a by-product in this equation, stands out as
one of the most controversial, misunderstood, and abused
topics within the church. It has left many Christians confused
and ill-informed about the subject. Yet, I am fully convinced
that money holds great importance to God. *How do I know?*
Money, along with its various forms, such as wealth, riches,

gold, cattle, and inheritance, is mentioned in well over two thousand verses throughout the Bible. Almost one-third (eleven out of the thirty-nine) of the parables Jesus taught in His earthly ministry pertain to money. If it holds such significance to God, as evidenced by His word, then it should also be important to the body of Christ.

Money is not only one of the most discussed topics in Scripture, but it also comes with the most warnings. An unhealthy relationship with money can be costly. Hence, it is essential to have a well-informed and balanced understanding to form the right perspective—a godly perspective. Renewing our minds about money is crucial for experiencing the necessary transformation within ourselves and impacting the world through our finances.

## A FINISHED WORK PERSPECTIVE

There are several commendable books on the subject of money available in the market, offering insights from both biblical and secular perspectives. However, only few have explored the topic through the lens of the finished work of Christ on the cross. The gospel establishes a new standard for our approach to viewing, requesting, receiving, and utilizing money—all from the perspectives of the Kingdom and new creation realities. Below are some of these perspectives.

> **Poverty or lack has already been dealt with on the cross.**

## MONEY AFTER THE CROSS

Adopting a post-cross perspective on money requires, above all, the understanding that poverty or lack has already been dealt with on the cross. Poverty is a curse, and Christ has borne all our curses. In the epistles, Paul explains that in Christ, we lack nothing: "For you know the grace of our Lord Jesus Christ, that though He was rich, yet for your sakes He became poor, **that you through His poverty might become rich**" (2 Corinthians 8:9, NKJV, emphasis added).

The root Greek word for "rich" in this verse, *ploutizō* [Strong's G4148], can be interpreted both *literally* as earthly riches or finances (2 Corinthians 9:11) and *metaphorically* as spiritual "enrichment" (1 Corinthians 1:4-5), with both uses found in the Bible. From this, we can gain a balanced insight and understanding into the word "enrichment" as signifying a form of completeness with permanent results.

**We are complete in Christ beyond earthly riches and blessings, with a completeness that bears eternal significance.**

Essentially, we are complete in Christ beyond earthly riches and blessings, with a completeness that bears eternal significance.

Consequently, our approach to money does not stem from a mindset of scarcity or the belief that "there is not enough." In the Kingdom, lack is nonexistent; there is an unending supply from an inexhaustible Source. In the spiritual realm, we have access to everything we need in Christ. Thus, we operate from a place of abundance and provision, not in pursuit of it. The notion of scarcity is merely an illusion, a lie. This understanding allows us to cease from striving and find rest in Christ's finished work. As John Crowder puts it brilliantly, "The people lack nothing, except a realization of what they already possess. It is finished. Everything is finished."[2]

This does not imply that all believers will be wealthy, nor does it suggest that we will never face financial challenges. However, the enduring truth is that we have completeness in Christ and lack nothing. Our experiences do not change this truth; rather, the truth has the power to transform our circumstances as we stand firm in faith.

Embracing a post-cross perspective also alters how we approach God about money, leading us to a more effective form of prayer. Rather than regularly asking or pleading for money or provision, we give thanks for His provisions in faith, recognizing that in Christ, He has already provided for us abundantly—encompassing both earthly and spiritual blessings.

"His divine power has given to us **all things that pertain to life and godliness,** through the knowledge of Him who called us by glory and virtue." (1 Peter 1:3, NKJV)

Instead of worrying about provision, focus on discerning where He wants to place you. For where He assigns, He also provides.

Another post-cross perspective on money involves shifting our beliefs from viewing it as a product of mere human effort and willpower. This can take the form of "manipulating" or "bribing" God with the expectation of His financial blessings, either by observing the law and tithing under the old covenant—or by "mastering" Christian practices like sowing and reaping, its new covenant equivalent. Moreover, human effort can take the form of working very hard for money and attributing all success to our own abilities without acknowledging the Source. The cross has qualified us for God's provision as His children as we work diligently and in excellence.

## MONEY IN TWO ECONOMIES

We are all acquainted with the world's economy, experiencing its impact daily. Yet, how many of us truly understand heaven's (or God's) economy? And for those who do, how integrated is it into your everyday life? The extent to which it has permeated into your beliefs and mindset is the same extent to which it influences your day-to-day life. Unlike the tangible and measurable economic system of the world, heaven's economy is invisible, making it challenging to comprehend for the natural man. Yet, it is undeniably real—arguably more real than the cash in your hands. Because it exists in the spiritual realm, it can only be understood and perceived spiritually through the lens of faith. Faith is the currency of heaven.

> The Kingdom's economy is characterized by its abundance and unlimited resources, remaining ever immune to recession.

The world's economic system operates on limited resources, marked by experiences of economic highs (booms) and lows (downturns). On the other hand, the Kingdom's economy is characterized by its abundance and unlimited resources, remaining ever immune to recession. The world's economic system, grounded in scarcity, constantly demands our time, energy, and finances—it is always taking from us. In contrast, heaven's economic system is founded on God's lavish generosity and His desire to bless His children in accordance with His vast riches and glory in Christ Jesus (Philippians 4:19)—it is always giving.

Therefore, it is crucial to view money within the framework of heaven's economy, even as we participate in the world's economy. For the believer, heaven's economy transcends and supersedes that of the world's; we simply need to learn the ways and principles of the Kingdom and operate in them even when they defy the rules and standards of the world.

## MONEY AND MORALITY

Money, in and of itself, is *amoral*—neither inherently good nor evil. It is simply a tool. Much like a rock, it can be used to build or to destroy. Money can serve as a means to meet needs and wants, bless people, fund visions and dreams, lift communities out of poverty and restore their dignity, and revitalize cities and nations. Conversely, it can also become a tool to ensnare its owners, inflict harm or abuse on others, lord it over others, and advance evil. Ultimately, the choice of how you use your money lies with you!

Money simply reveals the heart condition of its owner. It only amplifies and magnifies the hidden intentions and unresolved (unhealed) issues of an individual. For example, people who struggle with feelings of rejection may use their money to seek or even demand acceptance. Similarly, those who experienced poverty in the past may exhibit extreme behaviors, such as frugality or hoarding, as a form of overprotection. They may also engage in overspending and pretentious display as a means of overcompensation. Money merely reflects the character of its possessor, highlighting its inherent amoral nature.

> Money is simply a tool . . . It only amplifies and magnifies the hidden intentions and unresolved (unhealed) issues of an individual.

However, the love of money is *immoral*. Scripture warns us that "the love of money is the root of all kinds of evil" (1 Timothy 6:10, NIV). This love of money appears to be a heart issue, does it not? It represents the unresolved heart issues (discussed above) that have evolved into belief systems, shaping an individual's mindset and manifesting through actions. Does this sound familiar? Yes, a poverty mindset! The love of money is, in essence, an expression of a poverty mindset. Thus, there arises a profound need for healing and the transformation of our mindset regarding money.

Money, unlike anything else, has the potential to rule our hearts. It gives us power and freedom like no other. This is why it stands as the only *major* master competing with God for our affection and loyalty, though other lesser entities can also become idols. Scripture cautions us that serving two masters is impossible (Matthew 6:24). We must choose between God and mammon (the name that personifies money as god). Devotion to one inevitably leads to the despise of the other. The love of money has the power to displace God's place in our hearts, slowly chipping away the love and zeal we once held for God and His ways. Left unchecked, this can diminish our spiritual sensitivity or even our faith itself.

So, what should be our stance towards money as believers? We now understand that money itself is not evil, but the love for it is. Does this insight encourage you to embrace money as a wonderful tool for all the good it can bring? Or does it instill a fear of it due to the potential temptations it may bring, stemming from unresolved issues within your heart?

Let me assure you of something: while having money (especially lots of it) may bring its own temptations, being in lack does not exempt you from them either. Those in poverty or lack are not immune to temptations such as dishonesty, theft, or dishonoring God's name. Similarly, those with riches face the temptations of arrogance and denying the Lord: "If I'm too full, I might get independent, saying, 'God? Who needs him?' If I'm poor, I might steal and dishonor the name of my God" (Proverbs 30:8-9, MSG).

Therefore, be wary of any doctrine that teaches money as evil and that equates poverty, or being in lack, with spirituality, holiness, or virtue. This mindset stems from a religious spirit! Remember, this contrasts with the virtues of self-control and contentment with money and possessions, which are indeed valuable and represent a great gain—they are the fruit of the Spirit. If poverty (lack) were truly virtuous, why would God instruct us to help the poor (anyone in need) and restore them to dignity? Would that not be a disservice to them?

> If poverty (lack) were truly virtuous, why would God instruct us to help the poor (anyone in need) and restore them to dignity?

These teachings have caused significant harm to the church. This distorted perception of money is costly and deprives us of the influence and impact we are called to have in the world through our finances. It has led to generations of indifferent Christians who are only surviving, barely making ends meet, and waiting for heaven. We are not only saved from sin and hell; we are saved for good works in this world.

"For we are his workmanship, created in Christ Jesus for good works, which God prepared beforehand, that we should walk in them." (Ephesians 2:10, ESV)

This Scripture is not only referring to the good works of verbally preaching the gospel, which is indeed important, but predominantly on demonstrating the gospel through our actions and deeds, both in small gestures or significant acts. And let us be clear, financial resources are necessary to fund all these endeavors!

Christ's finished work on the cross initiated the redemption and restoration of every facet of the fallen creation: "For in him [Jesus] all the fullness of God was pleased to dwell, and through him to **reconcile to himself all things, whether on** earth or in heaven, making peace by the blood of his cross" (Colossians 1:19–20, NIV, emphasis added). God actively governs all aspects of creation to showcase His glory and promote its well-being. However, we are active participants with Him in declaring, releasing, and activating this redemption. As the body of Christ, we are called to bring heaven on earth! This work of redemption demands our resources.

God has many dreams and plans for us to fulfill. Creation is in eager anticipation of our intervention to address significant problems and alleviate pain and suffering in the world through the power of the Holy Spirit. Some of us are called to birth organizations dedicated to fighting child and sex trafficking, others to promote justice and reconciliation in places where there is little or none, and still others to introduce godly and holistic education programs to children.

Some are destined to launch redemptive businesses that create ethical products to prevent or cure diseases, produce wholesome foods, invent redemptive technologies, serve overlooked and underserved communities and markets, disrupt corrupt corporations exploiting and oppressing people, and so much more. These assignments (missions) span across different industries and spheres of influence to which God has specifically called and assigned us. And all these endeavors require money!

## GOD OWNS ALL MONEY

God is the owner of all things—from the wild animals to every plant on the ground to every human on the face of the earth (Psalm 24:1). Even the silver and the gold are His (Haggai 2:8); all money belongs to Him. To frame it in today's context, whether it is money in the Federal Reserve (under government control), commercial banks, financial markets, or any other assets across the globe, it all falls under His ownership. Even the money in your bank account is His possession.

Having established God's sovereignty over all money, what, then, is our role? As Christians, we are often taught that we are stewards, not owners, of the financial resources God entrusts to us, which is a valid and true statement. However, allow me to interject a different perspective, which I believe is a higher revelation that supersedes this truth. Are we mere stewards or more? Has the cross not elevated our status, making us co-owners with Christ? This kind of ownership is different from that which is self-generated or self-claimed, which is grounded on our human efforts and achievements. It is distinct from the mindset that proclaims, "My power and the strength of my hands have produced this wealth for me." (Deuteronomy 8:17, NIV).

> **It is time to shift our perspective and elevate our thinking, moving beyond seeing ourselves merely as stewards managing God's resources, to embracing our position as co-owners with Christ . . . We are called to co-create, co-plan, co-build, and co-influence the world with Christ.**

If Christ indeed is the rightful owner of all things, both in heaven and on earth, and the cross has made us joint-heirs with Christ to the inheritances of the Kingdom, then does this not mean that we are co-owners with God, inheriting His wealth, as we fully surrender to Him?

"And since we are his true children, we qualify to share all his treasures, for indeed, we are heirs of God himself. And since we are joined to Christ, we also inherit all that he is and all that he has." (Romans 8:17-18, TPT)

"Now we're no longer living like slaves under the law, but we enjoy being God's very own sons and daughters! And because we're his, we can access everything our Father has—for we are heirs because of what God has done!" (Galatians 4:7, TPT)

It is time to shift our perspective and elevate our thinking, moving beyond seeing ourselves merely as stewards managing God's resources, to embracing our position as co-owners with Christ. As such, we are called to co-create, co-plan, co-build, and co-influence the world with Christ.

## GOD GIVES WEALTH

True wealth originates from God. Scripture describes it like this: "When God gives someone wealth and possessions, and the ability to enjoy them, to accept their lot and be happy in their toil—this is a gift of God" (Ecclesiastes 5:19, NIV). Unlike wealth acquired through dishonest and corrupt methods, this represents a blessing from God (Proverbs 10:22). It emerges as a natural by-product of making God and His Kingdom our first priority in every aspect of life, work included.

Contrary to common belief, while God remains the ultimate provider, He does not give us wealth or money directly (excluding inheritances from family and gifts from others). Instead, He gives us the ability and power to produce wealth (Deuteronomy 8:18). Merely asking God for wealth (or provision) in prayer, often without taking action in faith or engaging in productive activities, will not usher us into His abundance. God blesses the work of our hands (Deuteronomy 28:12), not mere intentions or unactioned ideas. Faith that is not activated and applied through works is not truly faith; it is simply hope.

Additionally, true riches are not accompanied by sorrow (Proverbs 10:22). They are free from the painful toil, which is evident in wealth that is solely self-sourced and self-willed and does not have its origins in God. Wealth that is amassed through blood, sweat, and striving requires the same level of effort to sustain. In contrast, the blessings that come from God are marked with ease and effortlessness; they are infused with God's anointing.

## MONEY HAS A PURPOSE

The money that God provides serves a purpose. As noted earlier, money is simply a tool. Some people mistake it as an indicator of achievement or becoming someone of significance; however, money itself should never be the end goal. It is the means to a goal. I am convinced that God blesses us with money for five primary reasons:

### 1. Needs.

We all require food, shelter, and clothing. In such cases, money serves as a tool to fulfill our needs. Just as any caring father provides for his children's needs, our heavenly Father, from His goodness and abundance, will also "liberally supply [fill until full] our every need according to His riches in glory in Christ Jesus" (Philippians 4:19, AMP).

### 2. Dreams and Visions.

Money acts as a facilitator for fulfilling not only our dreams and visions but also those of others. For those who are aligned with their God-given dreams and visions, God ensures the provision of necessary funds.

"God is able to make all grace abound to you, **so that having all sufficiency in all things at all times, you may**

**abound in every good work."** (2 Corinthians 9:8, ESV, emphasis added)

Discovering our God-given purpose, calling, or assignment is paramount for accessing this provision. Whether you currently have the financial means or are relying on God to supply as you proceed, venture into your dreams with the Holy Spirit's guidance and steadfast perseverance. Go ahead and write the book God has inspired within you. Launch the business you have long dreamed of or envisioned. Start the non-profit or ministry that burdens your heart. Invent the product you have been contemplating. Record the song that plays in your soul. Whatever your assignment or calling, proceed with co-creating and co-building your vision with Jesus while seeking His provision.

## 3. Charity.

Money serves as a means to bless others, whether through our contributions to the church for missions, helping someone in need, or supporting an organization's cause. It is impossible to grow in our knowledge and love of Jesus and not simultaneously grow in our generosity. As we come to know Him more intimately, we become more like Him. Partaking in His generous nature enables us to extend the same generosity and love to those in need—regardless of the size of our contribution—in accordance with what we have received. Consequently, God tends to continually bless those who are conduits of His generosity, passing on the blessings to others rather than those who hoard.

> It is impossible to grow in our knowledge and love of Jesus and not simultaneously grow in our generosity.

"Every man shall give as he is able, according to the blessing of the Lord your God that he has given you." (Deuteronomy 16:17, ESV)

"Whoever is generous to the poor lends to the LORD, and he will repay him for his deed." (Proverbs 19:17, ESV)

"A generous person will prosper; whoever refreshes others will be refreshed." (Proverbs 11:25, NIV)

**4. Influence.**
Money transforms into a tool for creating a larger societal impact. It offers a unique form of power unlike any other—affluence is for influence. A godly person can harness this power wisely for positive change across various spheres of influence. As believers, our impact should extend beyond the four walls of the church and into the nations. Outside the church confines, the key domains for impact, also known as the seven mountains of influence, include business, arts and entertainment, media, government, family, education, and religion. Leverage your wealth for the glory of God!

**5. Pleasure.**
Money is a tool meant to bring us joy. God blesses us with financial resources for our pleasure. Scripture encourages us to delight in a Father "who richly provides us with everything for our enjoyment" (1 Timothy 6:17, NIV). A good Father delights in seeing His children rest and relax, savoring life's many blessings.

**MONEY AND FAITHFULNESS**
True wealth is a function of faithfulness in the Kingdom. Faith-

fulness leads to abundance and multiplication. Those who value and use their blessings and gifts from God wisely and with integrity, regardless of their size, are entrusted with more. Conversely, those who neglect or devalue their divine blessings and gifts risk losing even what they possess (Matthew 25:29). It will be reallocated to the faithful who will utilize them effectively.

As an attribute of God, faithfulness also positions us for His promotion. A trustworthy person not only effectively manages their own possessions but also stewards with integrity what belongs to others. Consequently, they are entrusted with greater responsibility. In the Parable of the Talents, the master rewarded the faithful servant, saying, "Well done, good and faithful servant. You have been faithful and trustworthy over a little, **I will put you in charge of many things; share in the joy of your master**" (Matthew 25:23, NIV, emphasis added). Are you being faithful with the gifts you have received?

## MONEY AND WORK

There exists a positive correlation between money and work. We have previously established that true wealth is the product of God blessing the work of our hands. Scripture affirms this truth, saying, "The Lord will open to you his good treasury, the heavens, **to give the rain to your land in its season and to bless all the work of your hands**" (Deuteronomy 28:12, ESV, emphasis added).

Contrary to popular beliefs even among believers, work is not cursed. God Himself engages in work. Work existed before humanity's fall. In the Garden of Eden, the ground willingly yielded its fruit to man, making work enjoyable. However, after the fall—as a consequence of Adam's actions—God cursed the ground, decreeing that man would only eat from it through painful toil, yielding "thorns and thistles" instead of fruitful yields (Genesis 3:17-18). Thus lies the basis for the common perception that work is cursed. However, there is good news! The cross has reversed the curse:

"Christ purchased our freedom and redeemed us from the curse of the Law and its condemnation by becoming a curse for us." (Galatians 3:13, AMP)

With Jesus, the second Adam, we now experience a renewed relationship with work. Yet, this does not imply that we are immune to challenges or failures even as we pursue our dreams and visions and undertake meaningful work.

> We no longer work from a position of toiling and slaving away; rather, we work from a place of rest. We work diligently, yet with ease and anointing as we assume the positions God leads us into.

So, what does a healthy relationship with work entail after the cross? As believers under the new covenant, what perspective should we hold towards work?

First, work is now blessed! It is inherently good, no matter how menial or lofty. With this renewed perspective, we can begin to find joy in our work. Even how we work has been redeemed. We no longer work from a position of toiling and slaving away; rather, we work from a place of rest. We work diligently, yet with ease and anointing as we assume the positions God leads us into. We work in tandem with the flow and guidance of the Holy Spirit. Again, this does not exempt us from setbacks and heartaches at times.

Second, our work is our ministry. Contrary to traditional definitions, ministry is not limited to the confines of a church or a designated mission field. Our ministry is wherever God has positioned us—be it in business, government, church, or even in our households. In this regard, work becomes an outlet where God is uniquely expressed through our personalities, talents, skills, and gifts. It is the place where God's creativity, wisdom, and power flow through us, offering solutions to real problems in the world. After all, we are the *imago Dei*—God's image bearers—recreated in Christ in His image and likeness for good works.

Third, our work must be an extension of our purpose, visions, and dreams. Except in periods of preparation and transition (regardless of their duration), our work should align with these elements. Such alignment is crucial for bearing much fruit in the world. It also leads to finding fulfillment in our work and a sense of meaning in life. If you find yourself miserable at work and dissatisfied with your tasks, this could be the reason.

> **Work becomes an outlet where God is uniquely expressed through our personalities, talents, skills, and gifts. It is the place where God's creativity, wisdom, and power flow through us, offering solutions to real problems in the world.**

Fourth, our work is not primarily about earning money or becoming rich. We may find this challenging because many of us have been conditioned to think in this manner. While it is entirely reasonable to expect fair compensation for our work, making money should not be our primary motivation for working. Where God positions us, He also ensures provision; financial providence naturally accompanies our calling.

Finally, our work is not where we find our significance—our worth is found in Christ. It should not be a source of approval or validation from others, as doing so can lead to idolatry. Our identity is not derived from our profession; work should not define who we are. Instead, we approach our work from a position of acceptance, grounded in the understanding that we are already fully accepted and approved in Christ.

Adopting a renewed mind about work positions us well to receive God's blessings, both financially and beyond, through our work.

## MONEY AND WISDOM

In exploring the dynamics between wisdom and money, we discover that wisdom reigns supreme and holds a greater value than money: "For wisdom is more precious than rubies, and nothing you desire can compare with her" (Proverbs 8:11, NIV). Those who prioritize wisdom over money set themselves on a trajectory toward receiving God's blessings. It is indeed wisdom to value wisdom!

Wisdom often acts as a precondition for receiving wealth from God, especially in substantial amounts. Essentially, wisdom precedes God's abundant blessings, making money a by-product of wisdom. In the book of Proverbs, wisdom proudly proclaims, "Riches and honor are with me, enduring wealth and righteousness" (Proverbs 8:18, NIV). It promises to bestow wealth upon those who cherish it, amply filling their treasuries (banks) (Proverbs 8:21).

The combination of wisdom and money creates a powerful duo. Paired together, they provide double protection in life against any form of temptation. Consider the immense good they can accomplish in this world for the glory of God.

"Wisdom along with an inheritance is good. And an [excellent] advantage for those who see the sun. For wisdom is a protection even as money is a protection,

But the [excellent] advantage of knowledge is that wisdom shields and preserves the lives of its possessors." (Ecclesiastes 7:11-12, AMP)

In times of financial prosperity, wisdom keeps us anchored. It ensures our focus remains on God rather than money, which can be transient. As our possessions increase, wisdom guards against arrogance and fosters humility. It instructs us to find our security in God, our true provider and the Source of true satisfaction, instead of the illusory stability offered by money. Without wisdom, we may declare, "'I am rich, I have prospered, and I need nothing,' not realizing that you are wretched, pitiable, poor, blind, and naked" (Revelations 3:17, ESV).

In times of scarcity, wisdom teaches us to live in contentment. True contentment and satisfaction are found in Christ alone. The Apostle Paul, in his wisdom, articulates this:

"I am not saying this because I am in need, for I have learned to be content whatever the circumstances. I know what it is to be in need, and I know what it is to have plenty." (Philippians 4:11-12, NIV)

Despite Paul's heritage of considerable wealth, privilege, and status, he regarded them insignificant compared to the supreme value, joy, and satisfaction found in knowing Christ Jesus.

## SYMPTOMS OF THE LOVE OF MONEY

As previously established, money itself is not evil; it is the love of money. God does not object to us possessing money; His concern is money dominating our hearts. The Amplified Bible describes the love of money in 1 Timothy 6:10 as "the greedy desire for money and the willingness to gain it unethically."

This love reveals the inclination of our hearts, our lust towards it. It is the reason we slave away and wear ourselves out in pursuit of riches.

Although not exhaustive, below is a list of indicators that suggest the love of money might be influencing someone's heart. These symptoms are not dictated by one's financial standing; even those with limited financial resources can exhibit these traits. Interestingly, you will find that the symptoms of the love of money mirror the characteristics of a poverty mindset.

## 1. Eagerness.

This represents an obsession with money, characterized by a compulsive and unhealthy longing for riches. While fantasizing about money may initially appear harmless to others, it can lead to greed if left unchecked.

> "But people who long to be rich fall into temptation and are trapped by many foolish and harmful desires that plunge them into ruin and destruction." (1 Timothy 6:9-10, NLT)

## 2. Greed.

This entails an intense and selfish craving for more money at the expense of others. If not addressed promptly, greed can cause us to overlook our values and compromise the well-being of others to satisfy the unquenchable, never-satisfied appetite for more. Ultimately, greed leads to dishonesty, corruption, or injustice.

> "The greedy bring ruin to their households, but the one who hates bribes will live." (Proverbs 15:27, NIV)

## 3. Selfishness.

This reflects an absence of empathy or indifference towards the poor or those in need. It is being overly concerned with one's advantage and needs only, even if it means disadvantaging someone else in the process.

> "But whoever has the world's goods (adequate resources), and sees his brother in need, but has no compassion for him, how does the love of God live in him?" (1 John 3:17, AMP)

## 4. Stinginess.

This manifests as a reluctance to give—showing a lack of willingness to support the church, God's work, and those in need. It is adopting the posture of a clenched fist when opportunities arise to give.

> "A stingy man hastens after wealth and does not know that poverty will come upon him." (Proverbs 28:22, ESV)

## 5. Hoarding.

This represents an obsession with accumulating money and possessions, ranging from subtle to extreme behaviors. Sooner or later, hoarding leads to disaster for the owner.

> "I have seen a grievous evil under the sun: wealth hoarded to the harm of its owners." (Ecclesiastes 5:13, NIV)

## 6. Arrogance.

This is conceit based on one's wealth and possessions. It is experiencing a sense of superiority over others or harboring contempt for those deemed unworthy or inferior.

"Instruct those who are rich in this present world not to be conceited or to fix their hope on the uncertainty of riches, but on God, who richly supplies us with all things to enjoy." (1 Timothy 6:17, NIV)

Distinguish between the love of money and true wealth—money that is acquired with integrity and used wisely for the glory of God, whether for our personal use or in service for others. Overlooking this distinction could prove costly! We must commit to transforming our thinking, viewing money through the lens of the Kingdom rather than the world's perspective. Let go of any religious misconceptions and embrace a post-cross, redemption-centered view of money. As we grow in this understanding, placing our confidence in His abundant nature rather than merely our own efforts for security, we inevitably lean into a wealth mindset.

Our foundation should be built on a strong understanding of our role as co-owners (co-heirs) with Christ of the inheritances of the Kingdom, with access to heaven's limitless resources. Armed with this knowledge, we are empowered to use our resources for advancing God's Kingdom—bringing heaven on earth in every circumstance.

In the next chapter, we will come full circle, affirming the reality of your inheritance of a wealth mindset in Christ. We will conclude the book with encouragement and practical applications to empower your journey.

# PART 3

# EXPERIENCE

## CHAPTER 9

# You Have Already Arrived!

"His divine power has granted to us all things that pertain to life
and godliness, through the knowledge of him who called us to
his own glory and excellence, by which he has granted to us his
precious and very great promises, **so that through them you may
become partakers of the divine nature**, having escaped from the
corruption that is in the world because of sinful desire."

2 PETER 1:3-4, ESV, EMPHASIS ADDED

SOME YEARS AGO, the Holy Spirit highlighted this powerful
Scripture, and it profoundly shifted my perspective on the
dynamics of the Kingdom. As I reflected on it, a deeper revelation and understanding unfolded. He graciously presented me
with a beautiful analogy—a parable, if you will—to unravel
the profound mysteries and realities of the Kingdom. I hope
it resonates with you as strongly as it did with me!

## THE PARABLE OF THE WEALTHY INVESTOR

The Kingdom of God is like an exceedingly wealthy man who,

out of the abundance of his kindness, chose to generously invest a billion dollars in a severely poor and seemingly undeserving individual as a gift. What a lavish gift, would you not agree? The wealthy man presented this gift in the form of a check, which was deposited in a bank. Unfortunately, the poor man failed to withdraw any funds and merely retained the bank book (or bank card)—His guarantee for the deposit.

With his newfound billion dollars, he was now set for life! The blessing extended to his entire family, all thanks to this extraordinary gift. Possessing such immense wealth, he did not *need* to work again if he chose not to. This windfall allowed him the freedom to leave that unfulfilling job he kept solely to make ends meet. Perhaps now, he could resurrect the dreams that laid dormant in his heart, waiting to be pursued. It was an opportunity to delve into his life passions, desires, and long-neglected talents and gifts as he transitioned from a survival mode to a thriving one. The possibilities were endless for investing his money to fulfill his true potential. Despite the abundance of opportunities, he opted to keep the bank book in the drawer. Not only did he fail to grasp the value of the check (gift), but he also lacked the understanding of how to put it to use. In his ignorance, he regressed to his former way of life—engaging in toil and striving. He failed to capitalize on the lavish gift bestowed upon him.

Now, picture this: what if, instead of investing (putting the money to work) and enriching his life, he went back to the wealthy man every time he had a need and consistently asked or pleaded whenever bills arose or expenses needed covering? How would you expect the wealthy man to respond?

One might anticipate a reply along the lines of, "What have you done with the money I already entrusted to you?" or "Why are you not using the gift (funds) I gave you to cover your expenses?" It is reasonable to assume the wealthy man might be disheartened, frustrated even, by the missed opportunity to make the most of the lavish gift he generously granted. After all, he made considerable sacrifices to bestow this unmerited gift upon the man and yet it remains untouched. The expectation was that he would utilize this gift to enhance and embrace his best life, thriving and bearing fruit.

The vision was for him to lead a fulfilled and prosperous life, becoming a generous giver and a source of blessings to others. Instead, he chose to neglect the gift and persistently turned to the wealthy man for every need. He continued to request more, oblivious to the fact that he had already been endowed with *everything* he needed for his entire life. He persisted in living as if he were poor, like a pauper clinging to his old ways. This man still did not realize that he was wealthy!

## THE MORAL OF THE STORY

This parable serves as a vivid representation of the gospel. In this analogy, the wealthy man symbolizes God the Father, and the unparalleled gift is none other than Jesus Christ, accompanied by every spiritual and earthly blessing found in Him. The poor man is a reflection of us, who were once bankrupt in our previous condition, yet now recipients of the extravagant gift of Jesus Christ. Furthermore, he embodies the many believers who, though saved, have yet to grasp their authentic identity as the "wealthy" in Christ and their rightful position in the Kingdom of God. Their inheritance in Christ still remains unrealized.

You see, echoing the wisdom from the Scripture at the beginning of this chapter, God has already provided us with absolutely everything essential for life and godliness in Christ. Similar to how the wealthy man deposited the check in the bank, God has already deposited within us Christ and all other things necessary for life and godliness. In Christ, we already possess a complete, righteous, and enriched nature, lacking nothing. Our life should be rooted in this completeness, living from this place of abundance and not working toward it. The only way to access this abundance is by faith through a genuine and intimate experiential knowledge of Christ, who, by His own glory and excellence, has qualified us.

> In Christ, we already possess a complete, righteous, and enriched nature, lacking nothing.

Similar to how the wealthy man gave the gift in the form of a check rather than cash and was deposited in the bank, God makes all His blessings and provisions available in the spiritual realm in the form of promises (2 Peter 1:4). We engage with God through these promises, and we become participants of His divine nature. The check in the bank symbolizes the unseen and invisible realities of the spiritual realm, while cash signifies manifestations in the natural realm, ready to be utilized. Just as the deposited check needs to be cashed for it to be used, God's promises need to be actively engaged with and accessed through faith to find their fulfillment in our lives.

From God's perspective, He has abundantly provided everything you could ever need in Christ—all fully paid for on your behalf. The promises and benefits bestowed through His Son are securely stored in the spiritual places. In this realm, all things have already found their completion in Christ! Jesus' final words on the cross, "'It is finished!'" (John 19:30, NLT), marked the conclusion of His work and mission and the perfect fulfillment of the law. It is done! Past tense. Period. The check has already been granted and deposited!

What remains on our part is to cash in the deposited check and put it to good use—for His purposes, the good of the world, and our enjoyment. Just as the poor man did not withdraw the money and did not experience its wonderful benefits and impact on his life, the lack of manifestations of God's promises and our inheritances in the physical realm does not negate their presence. It just means that we have not accessed them. Therefore, we cannot solely rely on our natural senses and instincts. The physical manifestations—the tangible results—occur as we actively engage the promises with faith, operating from the standpoint of having already received them

> The gospel unfolds the story of a "wealthy" God who made us "wealthy" beyond our wildest imagination, means, or qualification . . . Christ has become our *net-worth!*

and not striving to earn them. In partnership with the Holy Spirit, we bring forth what is unseen into the seen realm.

The gospel unfolds the story of a "wealthy" God who made us "wealthy" beyond our wildest imagination, means, or qualification. It is a narrative about one, Christ Jesus, who drastically changed our position, elevating us from the lowly status of beggars to the exalted status of royalty. Christ has become our net-worth! This is the starting point and essence of a wealth mindset! Embracing it entails thinking, speaking, and behaving as those who are truly "wealthy." It is time to align our thoughts, words, and actions with our rich inheritance!

## APPLICATION

### 1. Appropriation.

We claim what is rightfully ours into our lives and the lives of those under our authority. We take God's collective and universal promises to our personal use. Legally and fairly, we take exclusive possession of our inheritances in Christ. We appropriate everything that Jesus has already paid for on the cross into our individual lives, making it truly ours. We withdraw from the deposited check to fulfill all our needs for life and godliness, mastering the skill of bringing them forth from the unseen to the seen.

> **We appropriate not as those who are passive and timid but as those who are confident and bold—the spiritually "violent."**

We appropriate not as those who are passive and timid but as those who are confident and bold—the spiritually "violent." For "from the days of John the Baptist until now **the kingdom of heaven suffers violent assault, and violent men seize it by force [as a precious prize]**" (Matthew 11:12, AMP, emphasis added). If you wonder who the spiritual "violent" are, they are the mature sons of God who will take the Kingdom by force and appropriate its realities for themselves, their families, communities, and nations.

They are the ones who will fight to seize God's promises—what is rightfully and legally theirs through Christ—snatching them from the enemy's hands. They are willing to press through and possess their inheritance in Christ, pulling down heaven's realities and culture into the earth. They are believers who will hold onto their faith and persevere through severe trials and sufferings and share in Christ's glory. They are the mature children of God that creation eagerly awaits their revelation (Romans 8:19). These are the believers with a wealth mindset!

### 2. Prayer.

There is a superior way to pray! We no longer pray as paupers but as the "wealthy" in Christ, as those who already possess all things in Him, even when our prayers have not resulted in their manifestations yet. We pray from a position of victory, abundance, and completeness.

When we pray, we shift our focus away from the present (our needs or current circumstances) and the future (our predictions and plans). Instead, we anchor ourselves in the past—the cross—where all things were accomplished, and our identity was established. It is the place where all things were made possible in Christ. Let the profound reality of the gospel shape not only our present but also our future!

**We pray from a position of victory, abundance, and completeness.**

Our prayer lives become tremendously transformed in light of the finished work of the cross. They become infused with gratitude and thankfulness. We no longer await the physical manifestation of our promises to praise and delight in God; in the spiritual realm, they are already a done deal!

> "For as many as are the promises of God, in Christ they are [all answered] 'Yes.' So through Him we say our "Amen" to the glory of God." (2 Corinthians 1:20, AMP)

All too often, our prayer life resembles the attitude and behavior of the poor man in the parable above. Unaware of what he already possessed, he repeatedly approached the wealthy man, beseeching and pleading for more (money) to meet his every need. He was oblivious to his already acquired wealth and secure future. If he truly grasped his value, each encounter with the wealthy man would be an opportunity for incessant, unrestrained gratitude.

Understanding our worth in Christ transforms our prayers into expressions of ceaseless appreciation and adoration, regardless of our circumstances. Rather than endless petitions or constant pleas for blessings, our prayer focus shifts to beholding His presence and contemplation of the cross, His nature, and our new identity in Christ. By abiding in His presence and drinking from His Spirit, we are filled, empowered and reminded of Kingdom realities. Our prayer mostly becomes an act of adoration and delight in Him, a characteristic trait of believers with a wealth mindset!

### 3. Mind Renewal.

The poor man lacked an awareness of what he had been given. He failed to grasp his worth and the value of the lavish gift that could change his life and the lives of those around him and beyond. Similarly, many believers fail to realize what they already possess in Christ. We lack nothing, everything we need (and will ever need) is found in Christ. We must live from the reality of the Kingdom within and not the world outside.

> **We must live from the reality of the Kingdom within and not the world outside.**

Christian maturity is about growing in the renewal of the mind. It is about continually awakening to the truth of what Christ has already accomplished. This mind renewal process is the only way to access the abundant life that Christ came to provide—a life that is rich, satisfying, eternal, and superior (John 10:10). It is the key to experiencing the Zoë life: the divine life that flows in and through us, bringing the fullness of His love, peace, joy, righteousness and power. In Christ, we already possess this Zoë life right now!

The renewed mind interprets all of life through the lens of the cross, rather than being shaped by past hurts and trauma, cultural influences, personal preferences and desires, or the opinions of others. It consistently taps into the mind of Christ, viewing God, oneself, and others from a Kingdom perspective. This renewed mind identifies and replaces the lies of the enemy with truth. It operates from a heavenly perspective to earthly matters, leading to a life that is fulfilling, prosperous, and fruitful in the Spirit. This is the essence of a wealth mindset!

## 4. Posture.

Our response to this completed work of Christ should be one of rest. Those who understand the essence of grace find their rest because its language is "done," as opposed to the legalistic language of "do." Our posture of rest mimics God's rest in His finished work.

> "God's rest celebrates his finished work; whoever enters into God's rest immediately abandons his own efforts to compliment what God has already perfected." (Hebrews 4:10, The Mirror)

Unlike the poor man in the parable who persisted in striving despite the abundance freely given to him, we rest from the demands of performance and striving. We cease from self-improvement or external behavior modification, allowing the transformative power of the gospel to shape and conform us to His image. We let grace work within us, bringing transformation from the inside out.

**Our posture of rest mimics God's rest in His finished work.**

True grace is not a license for sin or laziness; instead, it is an acknowledgment of Christ's completed work on the cross and a supernatural empowerment to live in our authentic identity in Christlikeness.

Above all, we rest from striving to earn God's grace—His lavish gift—through our works. We rest from attempting to contribute through our efforts to the already finished work of Christ and to what God has already perfected. Instead, we rest in the sufficiency of Christ, receiving freely and gratefully with child-like faith. We rest in God's love and goodness! A posture of rest marks the life of the believer with a wealth mindset.

## A FINAL WORD

I appreciate the journey we have taken together through our exploration of a Kingdom wealth mindset. I invite you to contemplate the truth presented in this book and continue renewing your mind with the good news of Jesus' finished work. Keep awakening to the mind of Christ within you, allowing His perspective to shape your thoughts and actions. Above all, I call on you to celebrate the cross because you have already arrived!

A wealth mindset is your birthright!

# Translation Index

Throughout *The Wealth Within*, the author references multiple Bible translations to help accurately convey the depth of meaning of various scriptures. The translations used can be identified by the following codes:

**AMP** - The Amplified Bible
**AMPC** - The Amplified Bible, Classic Edition
**ESV** - English Standard Version
**KJV** - King James Version
**MSG** - The Message Translation
**NIV** - New International Version
**NKJV** - New King James Version
**NLT** - New Living Translation
**TPT** - The Passion Translation
**The Mirror** - The Mirror Bible Translation

# End Notes

**CHAPTER 1**

1. Tzu, Lao. "A Quote by Lao Tzu." Goodreads. https://www.goodreads.com/quotes/8203490-watch-your-thoughts-they-become-your-words-watch-your-words.
2. Du Toit, Francois. 2018. *The Mirror Bible*. 8th ed.
3. Crowder, John. 2023. "If your idea of sovereignty involves God single-handedly causing everything, then you have collapsed God into creation—a reprehensible monism that posits all human evils and atrocities as actions and therefore attributes of the divine nature..." Facebook. https://www.facebook.com/thenewmystics.
4. Lewis, C. S. 2001. *Mere Christianity*. HarperOne. p. 48.

**CHAPTER 2**

1. Hull, Sharon. 2009. "Any Dream Worth Considering Is Worth Evaluating (and Tweeting?)." Uploaded by John Maxwell. *John Maxwell*. April 23, 2009. https://www.johnmaxwell.com/blog/any-dream-worth-considering-is-worth-evaluating-and-tweeting/.
2. Peale, Norman Vincent. 1956. The Power of Positive Thinking. Prentice Hall.

3.  "Fear." 2024. In *Cambridge Dictionary*. https://
    dictionary.cambridge.org/us/dictionary/english/fear.
4.  "Worry." In *Oxford Learner's Dictionary*. https://www
    .oxfordlearnersdictionaries.com/us/definition/english
    /worry_2.
5.  "Doubt." In *Oxford Learner's Dictionary*. https://www
    .oxfordlearnersdictionaries.com/us/definition/english
    /doubt_1?q=doubt.

**CHAPTER 3**

1.  "Strong's Concordance Hebrew and Greek Trans-
    literations." n.d. Blue Letter Bible. https://www
    .blueletterbible.org/.
2.  Twain, Mark, and Caroline Thomas Harnsberger. 2009.
    *Mark Twain at Your Fingertips*. Dover Publications. p.
    354. https://ci.nii.ac.jp/ncid/BA20076483.

**CHAPTER 4**

1.  Crowder, John. 2010. *Mystical Union*. Sons of Thunder
    Publications. https://www.johncrowder.net/products
    /mystical-union. p. 71.
2.  Jimenez, Schlyce. 2018. *The Path: Journey With God
    and Live Your Purpose*. Edited by Anna Paradox. 2nd
    ed. Difference Press. p. 93. https://www.schlyce.com/wp
    -content/uploads/2018/04/The-Path.pdf.
3.  Spurgeon, Charles. 1871. "The Fourfold Treasure."
    *The Spurgeon Center*. Newington, London, United
    Kingdom of Great Britain and Northern Ireland, April
    26. https://www.spurgeon.org/resource-library/sermons
    /the-fourfold-treasure/#flipbook/.
4.  Munroe, Myles. 2006. *Kingdom Principles*. Destiny
    Image Publishers. p. 16.

5. Ibid., pp. 18-19.
6. Jenkins, Amanda, Kristen Hendricks, and Dallas Jenkins. 2019. *The Chosen: 40 Days with Jesus*. Broad-Street Publishing Group LLC. Entry of July 25, 2020.

## CHAPTER 5

1. Piper, John. 2012. "God Is Most Glorified in Us When We Are Most Satisfied in Him." Desiring God. October 13, 2012. https://www.desiringgod.org/messages/god-is -most-glorified-in-us-when-we-are-most-satisfied-in-him.
2. Johnson, Bill. "God Is Good – Bill Johnson Ministries." n.d. https://bjm.org/core-values/god-is-good/.
3. Johnson, Bill quoted in Ellis, Paul. 2016. "Bill Johnson on the Goodness of God." Escape to Reality. November 23, 2016. https://escapetoreality.org/2010/08/29/bill -johnson-on-the-goodness-of-god/.
4. Crowder, John. 2010. *Mystical Union*. Sons of Thunder Publications. p. 176.
5. Evans, Tony. "Seeing God's Provision." Sermon; March 27, 2023. https://sermons.love/tony-evans/386-tony -evans-seeing-gods-provision.html.

## CHAPTER 6

1. Vallotton, Kris. "A Quote by Kris Vallotton." Facebook. Sept 3, 2020. https://www.facebook.com/kvministries.
2. Crowder, John. 2010. *Mystical Union*. Sons of Thunder Publications. p. 130.
3. Du Toit, Francois. "A Quote by Francois Du Toit." Facebook. Nov 13, 2022. https://www.facebook.com /francois.toit.
4. Lewis, C. S. quoted in Crowder, John. 2010. *Mystical Union*. Sons of Thunder Publications.

5. Johnson, Bill. 2006. *Dreaming with God*. Destiny Image Incorporated. p. 88.
6. Munroe, Myles. 2006. *Kingdom Principles*. Destiny Image Publishers. p. 52.
7. Ibid., p. 53.
8. Spurgeon, Charles Haddon. 1990. *Morning and Evening*. The Old-Time Gospel Hour. p. 408.
9. Crowder, John. 2010. *Mystical Union*. 2010. Sons of Thunder Publications. p. 83.

**CHAPTER 7**

1. Baker, James. "Wealth with God by James Baker." Facebook. March 14, 2024. https://www.facebook.com /WealthWithGod.
2. Hugo, Victor. (1862) 2015. *Les Miserables*: (Penguin Classics Deluxe Edition). Penguin. p. 173.

**CHAPTER 8**

1. Baker, James. "Wealth with God by James Baker." Facebook. https://www.facebook.com/WealthWithGod.
2. Crowder, John. 2010. *Mystical Union*. Sons of Thunder Publications. p. 168.

www.ingramcontent.com/pod-product-compliance
Lightning Source LLC
Chambersburg PA
CBHW060918120626
46553CB00001B/364